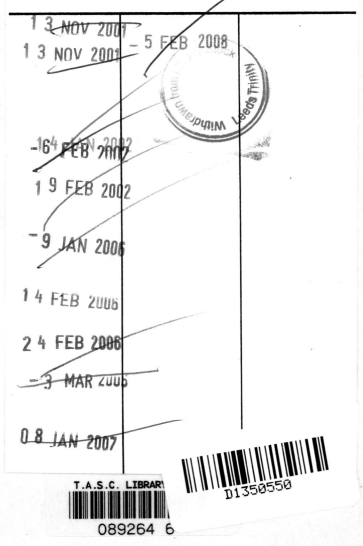
THE LO\
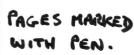

A View of S
History Pl

Edited by John Wilders

Samuel Butler: Hudibras, with an Introduction and Commentary (1967)
Shakespeare: The Merchant of Venice (Casebook series) (1969)

THE LOST GARDEN

A View of Shakespeare's English
and Roman History Plays

JOHN WILDERS

M

© John Wilders 1978

First published 1978 by
THE MACMILLAN PRESS LTD
London and Basingstoke
Associated companies in Delhi Dublin
Hong Kong Johannesburg Lagos Melbourne
New York Singapore and Tokyo

Photoset, printed and bound
in Great Britain by
REDWOOD BURN LIMITED,
Trowbridge and Esher

British Library Cataloguing in Publication Data

Wilders, John
   The lost garden.
   1. Shakespeare, William – Histories
   I. Title
   822.3′3   PR 2982

ISBN 0–333–24469–9
ISBN 0–333–24470–2 Pbk

Contents

The cover illustration, adapted from a fifteenth-century frontispiece to a manuscript of John Lydgate's *The Fall of Princes*, is reproduced by permission of the Curators of the Bodleian Library, Oxford. It depicts the expulsion of Adam and Eve from the Garden of Eden and the falls from power of various historical figures.

For Catherine
1956–1975

It was, after all, the Greeks who pioneered the writing of history as what it has so largely remained, an exercise in political ironics – an intelligible story of how men's action produces results other than intended.

J. G. A. POCOCK

Comfort's in heaven; and we are on the earth.

Richard II, II ii 78

Foreword

Every time Shakespeare wrote a play he set for himself a new kind of challenge with the result that each one is unique in style, construction, characterisation and dramatic effect. Not the least achievement of the history plays is their diversity. The uniqueness of each history play is, however, not my concern in this book, nor have I paid much attention to Shakespeare's development as a poet and dramatist. What I have tried to convey is my belief, based on my acquaintance with the plays as a reader, actor, theatregoer and teacher, that the mind which created all the history plays was guided by certain largely unchanging assumptions. Whether Shakespeare is portraying the struggle between the Greeks and Trojans, the conspiracy against Julius Caesar or the victory of Henry V at Agincourt, his imagination is, I believe, governed by a view of human nature which he held irrespective of the historical period he chose to depict. Shakespeare's view of human nature shaped his view of history and it is these two interrelated attitudes which I have tried to describe and illustrate in the following chapters.

His view of human nature appears as evidently in his tragedies and comedies as in his histories, and the contents of this book could well have been only part of a much larger work dealing with the entire canon. I have confined myself to the histories partly because I was unwilling to embark on a larger enterprise and partly because these plays seemed to me in need of a fresh appraisal. Interpretation of the English histories has been and still is very strongly influenced by E. M. W. Tillyard's *Shakespeare's History Plays* (1944), even though it was published over thirty years ago and in spite of the challenges it has received from Wilbur Sanders, Robert Ornstein, H. A. Kelly and others. Tillyard's account of these plays can be found not only in his own writings but in such influential places as the standard editions of

Shakespeare, discussions of his historical sources and many otherwise admirable works of criticism. I believe, however, that Tillyard seriously misinterpreted the plays and oversimplified the opinions of the chroniclers. Even if readers are unconvinced by my own arguments, I hope they may be encouraged to think again about assumptions which have long been widely accepted.

The effect of Tillyard's book has also been to separate the English histories from the rest of Shakespeare's work by creating the impression that, in writing them, he ceased for the time being to engage in the free-ranging speculations he conducted elsewhere in order to assume a much more rigid, official position, a 'Tudor' view of history which has no connection with the attitudes implicit in the tragedies and Roman plays. One of my purposes has been to establish the connections between the English and Roman histories and their connections with the tragedies, and thereby to restore the English histories to their place in Shakespeare's writings as a whole.

As each of the following chapters took shape I was reassured to discover that Shakespeare's ideas were often similar to those of his predecessors and contemporaries. I am not thinking of the chroniclers but of more profoundly influential writers such as St Augustine, Boethius, Calvin, Machiavelli and Montaigne. My treatment of Shakespeare could well have been prefaced by an account of his philosophical and theological 'background', but I have preferred to allude to these authors only occasionally when their ideas seemed to me relevant and to offer some explanation why the dramatist thought as he did. Any reader who is curious to trace Shakespeare's ideas to their sources should consult Hiram Haydn's *The Counter-Renaissance* (New York, 1950) which describes an 'Elizabethan World Picture' very different from Tillyard's, in which Shakespeare's intellectual predecessors are shown to have been sceptical and uncertain, conscious of their ignorance of God and man, living in a universe characterised not by its stability and order but by its innate tendency towards chaos.

My best teachers have been my pupils and I am indebted to the students at the universities of Princeton, Bristol, Oxford and California for their insights and the good-natured challenges they have given me. I have acknowledged my debts to the scholars and critics of whose ideas I have consciously made use, but no doubt I have failed to mention others who have influenced me in ways I can no longer recall. To those who find their ideas repeated here without acknowledgement, I offer my apologies and gratitude.

This book would probably not have been written had it not been for the generosity of my colleagues at Worcester College, Oxford, in allowing me a year's leave, and of the Australian National University in awarding me a Visiting Fellowship at their Humanities Research Centre where I was able to work without interruption and in very favourable conditions. I am particularly grateful to the Director of the Centre, Professor Ian Donaldson, and to Professor S. L. Goldberg of the History of Ideas Unit for their criticism and encouragement. I am also indebted to Dr Christopher Hill, the Master of Balliol, for helping me to place Shakespeare in his religious and philosophical context. If this book is intelligible it is largely because it has passed through the critical scrutiny of my wife who, with characteristic modesty, claims that if she can understand my prose, it must be intelligible to anyone.

The book is dedicated to the memory of our daughter Catherine who, had she lived, would have been a university student of English literature at the time I wrote it.

JOHN WILDERS

Note on References
References to Shakespeare's text are to Peter Alexander's edition of *The Complete Works* (London and Glasgow: Collins, 1951).

1 | *History and Tragedy*

When, after Shakespeare's death, John Heminge and Henry Condell, two of his former colleagues in the theatrical company for which he had written, gathered his plays together in the first collected edition of his dramatic works (the First Folio of 1623), they divided them into three kinds, comedies, histories and tragedies. On what principles they decided to include a play in one of these three sections we do not know; the fact that they placed *Cymbeline* among the tragedies suggests that their decisions were rough and ready and that they had no very scholarly interest in questions of genre.[1] The only immediately obvious feature which the histories have in common is that they all deal with the history of England. A case could be made for describing some of Heminge's and Condell's 'histories' as 'tragedies', particularly *Richard II* and *Richard III*, both of which have dominant heroes and are distinguished from the other histories in the table of contents by the description 'The Life and Death'. Again, some of the Folio tragedies could well be considered histories: *Julius Caesar* has no central, commanding hero of the magnitude of Hamlet or Macbeth and this play, too, is described as 'The Life and Death' of Julius Caesar. The superficial evidence suggests, then, that the distinction between Shakespeare's histories and his tragedies is not as clear-cut as the Folio division implies. Further evidence shows that the two sets of plays are very closely related.

It has been suggested that whereas the history plays are concerned with a character's political life, the tragedies deal with private relationships. This is the distinction proposed by Lily B. Campbell, who argues that, for Shakespeare, there was a difference between 'private and political virtue, which marked the difference between the realms of ethics and politics'. 'Tragedy', she concludes, 'deals with an ethical world; history with a political world.'[2] Both the histories and the Roman plays, however, present their major characters to us as much in private, domestic situations as in public, official roles. Prince Hal is shown in the tavern with Falstaff before he appears as King, negotiating with ambassadors or addressing his troops; Hotspur appears in domestic scenes with his wife as well as on the battlefield, and Coriolanus's relationship with his mother does much to explain his behaviour towards the Roman populace.

The reason for this combination of private and public situations in the history plays is that, for Shakespeare, the history of a nation is shaped by small groups of individuals placed in positions where they can control it, and its course is therefore determined by the distinctive personalities of these people and their relationships with one another. The causes of national unity or division, of prosperity or decline are, in Shakespeare's view, to be found not, as some of the fifteenth-century chroniclers had believed, in the providential power of God,[3] nor, as we are now inclined to think, in social and economic conditions, but in the temperaments of national leaders and their reactions towards one another. To understand the course of history we must understand these men, and their characters reveal themselves more vividly in intimate, private situations than in the council-chamber or the market place. This was a belief which Shakespeare shared with his greatest collaborator, the Greek historian Plutarch, who declared in the preface to his Lives of Alexander and Caesar:

> My intent is not to write histories but only lives. For, the noblest deedes doe not always shew mens vertues and vices, but oftentimes a light occasion, a word, or some sporte makes mens naturall dispositions and maners appeare more plaine, then the famous battells wonne, wherein are slaine ten thousand men, or the great armies, or cities wonne by siege or assault.[4]

Hence the process which leads to the assassination of Julius Caesar begins with a secret conversation between two friends, Brutus and Cassius, while a public event (the offer of a crown to Caesar) takes place off-stage; Henry V's ascent to political success begins with a quiet scene between himself and Falstaff in the back room of a tavern, and while Coriolanus is fighting the Volscians, his mother explains to his wife how she made him into a great soldier.

In the minds of Shakespeare's historical characters, personal and political motives are so combined and confused as to be inseparable.[5] Suffolk arranges Henry VI's marriage to Margaret of Anjou not simply because he hopes to rule the country by influencing her, but because he is in love with her and plans to have her close to him;[6] Hotspur joins the rebels against Henry IV not, in the first place, because he supports Mortimer's claim to the throne, but because he has just had a row with Henry and is incensed against him; Cassius starts the conspiracy against Caesar not simply because he sees him as a political tyrant but because he despises Caesar's physical frailty and is a better swimmer. As the Roman citizens well know, Coriolanus's military success is the result of personal as well as public motives:

> Though soft-conscienc'd men can be content to say it was for his country, he did it to please his mother and to be partly proud, which he is, even to the altitude of his virtue. (I i 35–9)

Another reason for this combination of motives is that in Shakespeare's plays (as in historical fact) fifteenth-century politics is a family affair. All the major characters in *Richard II* are descended from one ancestor, Edward III, and when Richard seizes Bolingbroke's inheritance, he seizes the lands and wealth which his own cousin should rightly have inherited from his uncle; the Wars of the Roses are fought between two related families, those of York and Lancaster, and the leaders on both sides – York and his four sons, Henry VI and his Queen – are intimately related by blood or marriage; the debate among the Trojan leaders about the continuation of the war (*Troilus and Cressida*, II ii) is a discussion between a father, Priam, and his sons. The political disasters of the history plays are made human and vivid because they are shown as personal disasters: when the English forces are defeated by the French in *Henry VI*, we see their leader, Talbot, holding his dead son in his arms; when Prince Hal makes his exit to become Henry V, he casts aside his old companion Falstaff; Caesar's dying words express his feeling of betrayal by a friend.

To this extent at least, Shakespeare's history plays resemble his tragedies in that a man's public life cannot be separated from his private life. Lily B. Campbell's distinction between the two modes is a false one, an attempt to parcel out the ground where the two dramatic forms actually overlap.

The plays collected in the Folio as 'Tragedies' also resemble those described as 'Histories' in that nearly all of them are based on what Shakespeare believed to be historical fact. The three major Roman plays are derived from the historical biographies of Plutarch, and the material for *Macbeth* and the main plot of *King Lear* is taken from the same source as the histories, the *Chronicles* of Holinshed. Even that tragedy within a tragedy, 'The Murder of Gonzago', is, Hamlet assures his audience, an image of an actual murder done in Vienna. In drawing on the historians for the material of his tragedies, Shakespeare, whether he knew it or not, was following the long-established literary principle that whereas the characters and plots of comedy are invented out of the poet's imagination, those of tragedy are usually based on historical fact. This principle, which originated in a misunderstanding of part of the ninth book of Aristotle's *Poetics*,[7] was given general currency by the fourth-century scholar Evanthius, whose essay *De Comedia* (ascribed by the Elizabethans to Donatus) was published as a preface to the early editions of the comedies of Terence. Evanthius makes several distinctions between comedy and tragedy, one of which is that comedies always have fictional plots whereas tragedies are often based on historical events.[8] It is probably because Evanthius's essay was so well-known and influential (Terence's comedies were a basic text in medieval and renaissance schools) that the idea reappeared in the treatises of many renaissance literary theorists. Scaliger, for example, states in his *Poetice* (1561) that 'comedy differs from tragedy in that, while the latter takes both its subject-matter and its chief names from history, such as Agamemnon, Hercules and Hecuba, in comedy all is fictitious'.[9] Castelvetro makes a similar point: 'The plots of all tragedies and all epics are and should be composed of happenings that can be called historical' whereas the comic poet 'gives no part to actual events or to history'.[10] The idea was so widespread in Shakespeare's time that he was probably acquainted with it, if not from a printed source then from the instruction he received from Thomas Jenkins, a graduate of St John's College, Oxford, and headmaster of the grammar school at Stratford-on-Avon which the dramatist almost certainly attended as a boy. But whether Shakespeare wrote with this principle in mind or not, it is a fact that his comedies are all based on fictional material and almost all (Evanthius's *saepe*) the tragedies are taken from recorded history. The only exceptions are *Romeo and Juliet* and *Othello*, the two domestic tragedies, and even these, with the feud between the Montagues and Capulets and the expedition against the Turks, have pseudo-historical backgrounds.

The close connection between Shakespeare's tragedies and his histories is further suggested by the disagreement among the early printers as to whether some of the plays belonged to one mode or the other.[11] Two of the plays included by Heminge and Condell in the Folio with the Histories, *Richard II* and *Richard III*, had been described as tragedies on the title-pages of the earlier quarto editions. There is, in fact, an inconsistency in the description of *Richard III* within the Folio itself: it is grouped with the histories and listed with them in the table of contents, but headed 'The Tragedy' on the first page of the text. Conversely, one of the folio tragedies, *King Lear*, had previously been entered in *The Stationers' Register* as 'the historye', and another, *Titus Andronicus*, as 'a Noble Roman Historye'. *Troilus and Cressida*, headed 'The Tragedie' on its opening page in the Folio, had been described as 'the history' in *The Stationers' Register* and the Quarto. This apparent uncertainty about the dramatic mode of certain plays may not be as significant as it seems at first sight since the term 'history' was not used precisely in Shakespeare's time. It could mean either 'a tale', 'a story' in a general sense, as in 'the most excellent Historie' of *The Merchant of Venice* (the Quarto title) or, more specifically, an account of events which are historically true, 'a chronicle history' as it was sometimes called. It is difficult to know in which sense the printers and the officials of the stationers' company used the word in relation to each play, but there is enough evidence to suggest that, when Shakespeare dramatised the narratives of Plutarch or the English chroniclers, his earliest readers were sometimes uncertain whether the completed plays were histories or tragedies.

The more one considers the question, the more difficult it becomes to define with any precision what, for Shakespeare and his contemporaries, distinguished his tragedies from his histories. This is partly, no doubt, because these men were not much concerned with exact distinctions. Moreover, whereas the theorists, from Aristotle onwards, had written at length about the nature of tragedy and comedy, there was no corresponding theory for the history play, a very recent form devised almost single-handed by Shakespeare himself whose histories have only the most superficial resemblance to such crudely moralistic works as *Gorboduc* and Bale's *King Johan*.[12] Since most of the tragedies are based on historical events, they are in this sense histories, though not all the history plays are tragedies.

The difference seems to lie in the role of the tragic hero. Whereas a history play portrays the fortunes of many characters as they play their roles in a nation's continuing life, a tragedy is devoted chiefly to the struggles of one character, and his death, depicted as the outcome of the conflicts which occupy the play, gives to the ending of a tragedy a sense of absolute finality. A Shakespearean tragedy has what Peter Ure calls 'the order and unity of biography',[13] a unity implied by the old title 'The Life and Death'. But whereas the death of a tragic hero conveys a sense of an ending, the impression created by a history play is that the life of a nation has neither beginning nor ending. It presents what Susanne Langer calls 'an incident in the undying life of a society that meets good and evil fortunes on countless occasions but never concludes its quest'.[14] This particular effect is discussed at length in the next chapter, but it may be sufficient to notice, for the time being, that *Henry VI Part I* ends with Suffolk's plans for the future (to rule Margaret and thereby to rule England), that *Henry IV Part II* ends with the first intimations of the invasion of France, and that *Julius Caesar* ends with the emergence of Antony and Octavius as the rulers of Rome. As Northrop Frye says,

> The emphasis and characteristic resolution of the history play are in terms of continuity . . . . *Richard II* and *Richard III* are tragedies insofar as they resolve on those defeated Kings; they are histories insofar as they resolve on Bolingbroke and Richmond, and the most one can say is that they lean toward history. *Hamlet* and *Macbeth* lean toward tragedy, but Fortinbras and Malcolm, the continuing characters, indicate the historical element in the tragic resolution. There seems to be a far less direct connection between history and comedy.[15]

Since, as Frye points out, indisputable tragedies contain 'continuing characters' and history plays like *Richard II* and *Henry IV* contain the tragedies of Richard, Hotspur and Henry, there are bound to be disagreements about where the line should be drawn, if anywhere. For the purposes of this book I have confined myself to the ten English and the three main Roman histories and *Troilus and Cressida*. This last work, incidentally, which has been variously described as a tragedy, a comedy, a history, a satire and a 'heroic farce' conveys more strongly than any other the sense of the continuing movement of history. It also contains the tragedy of Hector and, arguably, of Troilus.[16] Cases could be made for leaving out, say, *Richard II* as, strictly speaking, a tragedy or including the 'historical' tragedies *Macbeth* and *Hamlet*. My decision must be to some extent arbitrary for reasons already given.

I have suggested that, for Shakespeare, a man's public political life was in practice inseparable from his private life. Another way of putting this is to say that he conceived of history in terms of the lives of certain powerful individuals. Yet it is a distinguishing mark of a Shakespearean history play to portray the continuing life of a nation. Hence within the larger, continuing process of which each history play presents a part, the tragedies of certain individuals are contained. *Henry VI* contains the tragedies of Talbot, Gloucester, Suffolk, Warwick and York; *Henry IV* contains the tragedies of Hotspur and the King; *Julius Caesar* and *Troilus and Cressida* the tragedies of Caesar, Brutus and Hector. Like Plutarch, Shakespeare sees history in terms of 'lives'. These plays resemble those generally thought of as tragedies in that they portray the sufferings and deaths of these characters, but they differ from the tragedies in that their deaths do not form the culmination and conclusion of the plays (most of them occur anywhere but in the final scene). Hence the history plays invite us to observe the major characters from two points of view: that of the characters themselves as they struggle, like York and Richard III, to seize power, or, like Henry IV and Henry VI, to keep their country at peace, and the objective point of view of national or even world history which ironically reduces a character's significance in this larger context. The anxieties, achievements and death of a character in a Shakespearean history play are of the greatest importance to him but are of no great significance in the wider temporal context. The assassination of Julius Caesar and the Battle of Agincourt are shown to us as, at the same time, momentous and trivial, whereas in *King Lear* even the undoing of a button is charged with significance. This double view creates in an audience's mind an ambivalence which A. P. Rossiter (on evidence of a different kind) believed to be the distinguishing effect of the histories, a condition in which 'two opposed value-judgements are subsumed, and . . . both are valid'. Such a work, he continues, 'is only fully experienced when both opposites are held and included in a "two-eyed" view; and all "one-eyed" simplifications are not only falsifications; they amount to a denial of some part of the mystery of things'.[17]

The specific political problems portrayed in these plays were of the greatest interest to Shakespeare's contemporaries. The earliest histories are much concerned with the struggle between rival claimants to the throne, a problem which beset Elizabeth at the time of her accession and again in 1586 when the Babington Plot in support of Mary Queen of Scots was exposed. Emrys Jones has recently conjectured that the fears aroused by Mary's threat to Elizabeth gave a 'topical edge' to the three Parts of *Henry VI*.[18] Many of the histories depict the rise and fall of political adventurers such as Suffolk, York, Antony and Pompey, and such aspirants for power were familiar to audiences who had lived through Wyatt's plot against Queen Mary or the Essex rebellion. The transfer of power from Henry to Edward in *3 Henry VI* and from Richard to Bolingbroke in *Richard II* produces crises of loyalty in men like Warwick, York and Aumerle, and a nation which had had to reconsider its religious allegiances on the accession of the Protestant Elizabeth after the reign of the Catholic Mary had no doubt experienced similar crises; they were to occur again in the 1640s when Parliament demanded from Englishmen the allegiance they had formerly sworn to Charles I.

Nearly all the history plays, both English and Roman, are civil war plays portraying situations familiar to readers of the chroniclers on whose work Shakespeare drew and which consisted largely of accounts of rebellion and internal struggle. The problems in which Shakespeare's historical characters are engaged were the problems of his contemporaries. Yet I do not believe that Shakespeare wrote these plays as exemplary dramas, in the hope that the statesmen of his time would learn how to avoid the mistakes of their predecessors. It would not simply appear presumptuous for a journeyman playwright to advise statesmen and aristocrats like the Cecils on how to do their job, but it was also dangerous: a royal Proclamation of 1559 made it an offence punishable with imprisonment for plays to be performed 'wherein either matters of religion or of the governaunce of estate of the common weale shalbe handled or treated', the reason being that these were not the concern of the actors but only of 'menne of auctoritie, learning and wisdome'.[19] Moreover, since the peculiar combination of characters in a position to govern a country at one time is unique, every political problem is, in Shakespeare's view, unique. Henry IV's troubles in suppressing his former allies are quite different from Henry VI's in retaining the empire in France, and different again from Brutus's and Cassius's problems in dealing with a potential tyrant, or the uncertainties of the Trojans as they consider the value of the war in which they are engaged. For Shakespeare history does not repeat itself and therefore offers us no lessons of a practical kind. Sidney rebuked the man who believed he could find lessons in history, 'as if he should argue, because it rained yesterday, therefore it should raine to day'.[20] Nor do I believe that these plays are exemplary in a more general, ethical or religious sense. As Sidney also pointed out, 'history, being captived to the trueth of a foolish world, is many times a terror from well-doing, and an encouragement to unbridled wickedness';[21] as Bacon put it, history 'propoundeth the successes and issues of actions, not so agreeable to the merits of vertue and vice'.[22] Virtue is very seldom rewarded in the world of Lancastrian and Yorkist England, and the man who survives the contest of Roman politics is Octavius Caesar, a man not morally impeccable. The history plays portray what Samuel Johnson called 'the course of the world, in which the loss of one is the gain of another . . . and many mischiefs and many benefits are done and hindered without design'.[23]

If we can learn nothing from these plays about right political or moral conduct we may well wonder what assumptions Shakespeare brought to them, what transformations the narratives of Plutarch and the chroniclers underwent as they emerged as the Roman and English histories. They emerged chiefly as brilliantly constructed works for the theatre. The ability to arouse and control the responses of an audience was a skill which Shakespeare, the experienced professional actor, displayed even in the *Henry VI* plays.[24] They also emerged – and this is the subject of the following chapters – as the expression of a consistently held view of the human condition as one in which the solution of one problem creates problems of another kind, in which men thrive or suffer in ways which do not correspond to any ideal principles of justice, and choices are forced upon them, not between right and wrong, but between various courses of action all more or less unsatisfactory. Shakespeare's men of power, such as Richard III, Henry V and Coriolanus, are obviously possessed of heroic qualities: they are resourceful, courageous, capable of great endurance and assured of their capacity to shape the course of history in accordance with their own wills. The spectacle of such men in action is exhilarating. Yet Shakespeare's politicians seldom fulfil their ambitions and even if, like Henry V, they do succeed, their achievements are shown to be pitifully short-lived. Shakespeare portrays history as a struggle by succeeding generations of men to establish ideal worlds which are beyond their powers to create. Ideal societies are referred to from time to time as characters look back, like Humphrey of Gloucester, on the heroic age of Henry V, or, like John of Gaunt, on the vanished reign of Edward III, but the ideal kingdom is never to be found here and now:

'we have seen the best of our time'.

This discrepancy between an ideal past and a painful present, between the hopeful intentions of Shakespeare's heroes and their temporary, fragile achievements, is, I believe, a way of portraying in social and political terms the theological idea of a 'fallen' humanity. The myth of the Fall and the doctrines derived from it are an attempt to account for the imperfections of the secular world, for the way in which actual experience falls short of experience as we imagine, ideally, it could be. In the historical plays Shakespeare portrayed what Johnson described as 'the course of the world', 'the true state of sublunary nature' as he saw it. Shakespeare did not use the doctrines and terminology of the Fall to describe this world, but these doctrines – which, needless to say, were common knowledge to Shakespeare and his contemporaries – provide a fairly precise and systematic way of defining its characteristics: the temporal, shifting nature of man and his achievements, his subjection to the arbitrary whims of fortune, the separation between man and God and the hidden nature of God's purposes, man's ignorance of himself and of a world which had formerly been plain and clear to him, the impossibility of wholly right action in a creation which has become corrupt. Each of these ideas forms the subject of one of the following chapters.

I am as anxious to avoid creating the impression that Shakespeare was a consciously theological writer as I am to dispel the idea that he wrote exemplary history and, for this reason, I have not insisted that he had the specific doctrines of the Fall in mind as he wrote his plays. They were part of the instinctive way in which he looked at history. References to the Fall and its aftermath, however, will, I hope, provide a convenient framework for my discussion: they are an aid to defining the secularity of the history plays in precise terms. Shakespeare did not include much religious or theological discussion in his plays; the licensing laws of 1559 did not allow him to do so. As an Elizabethan Englishman, however, he could not have failed to be acquainted with the idea that man had once enjoyed a happy state in which his life was consistent with his hopes and he was free from the effects of time. Although Shakespeare's historical characters seldom talk theology, nevertheless the frustrations they experience and the defeats they suffer may be attributed to the constrictions imposed by God on mankind for Adam's disobedience. Conscious of the unsatisfactory nature of their times, they occasionally look back – or forward – to a golden age when things were better.

2 | *Time and Change*

'For eating the forbidden fruit of the tree of knowledge', says Raleigh, 'was Adam driven out of Paradise *in exilium vitae temporalis*, into the banishment of the temporal life.'[1] The history plays are recognisable generically by their emphasis on the continuing movement of time, and they convey in a variety of ways the experience of temporality, the bewilderment and frustration of people who find themselves in a world where nothing is permanent, and their attempts to withstand the effects of time. Our awareness of time depends entirely on our sense of change because it is through change that time reveals itself, whether in the movement of the fingers of a clock or the collapse of an empire. Drama is a form well suited to portraying the processes of time since performance has to take place within a certain more or less fixed period, and this sense of time passing is one of the resources of drama which Shakespeare exploits. An audience is made conscious, for example, of the prolongation of the suffering of Lear or Othello as it moves steadily towards its conclusion. They are not allowed the choice of avoiding any part of it, as we can by skipping the pages of a book or speeding up a tape recording.

Moreover the Elizabethan stage with its flexibility of place and the dramatic convention of short scenes enabled Shakespeare to make the lapse of time *between* scenes seem either short or long and thereby to create the illusion that time is passing either slowly or fast.[2] The periods of time which are assumed to have elapsed between the scenes leading up to the Battle of Agincourt are short, and hence time seems to drag slowly. As the location changes from the French to the English camp, the characters tell us the time of day and, though we cover a certain distance, the clock seems scarcely to move. In the middle of the French scene (III vii 87) we learn that it is midnight, and by the end of the scene that it is two o'clock in the morning; we hear later from the

Chorus that it is three o'clock, and dawn begins to break only after a large part of the English scene has been played (iv i 86). The conversation among the French leaders is, moreover, desultory and repetitive and this slowness of movement suggests a corresponding slowness of time. We therefore share with the characters the feeling that time moves slowly towards the day of the decisive battle. When Orleans complains 'Will it never be morning?', we share his impatience at being confined in 'the temporal life'. On the other hand, many days seem to have elapsed between the scene in *Antony and Cleopatra* (iii vi) where Octavius welcomes his sister on her return to Rome, and the one immediately following in which, only twenty lines later, he is said to have captured the town of Toryne. Antony, it is true, is astonished at his speed, but the rapid change in the military situation creates the illusion of a similarly quick passage of time. Moreover, since Antony cannot know what is happening outside Alexandria except from the reports of his messengers, his problems at this point in the play are those of a man confined in space, a limitation from which Octavius seems, miraculously, to be almost free. Antony lacks what in *Twelfth Night* is called 'that deity in nature of here and everywhere' (v i 219–20). Only Shakespeare knows what is happening everywhere in the play, but he shares some of his knowledge with the audience as he shifts the scene from place to place, and this privilege enables us to observe the difficulties which a character like Antony experiences simply because he is human.

Broadly speaking, Shakespeare depicts three different processes of time: the regular annual cycle of the seasons, or what the banished Duke in *As You Like It* calls 'the seasons' difference', one of the 'penalties of Adam' for his disobedience to God; the growth of the individual from birth to maturity and his decline to old age and death, feelingly expressed by Falstaff and another consequence of the Fall; and the random, irregular changes in society with its revolutions of government, victories and defeats in battle and shifts of popular allegiance. In the comedies the characters usually enjoy a respite from the demands of the last of these three processes because in Illyria or Arden or Messina they are members of very small, isolated societies and are free to give their whole attention to love and marriage. The dukes and kings of the early comedies, unlike their counterparts in the histories, seldom have armies to lead or subjects to govern. Social and political change is, however, a major subject of the histories: the formation and dissolution of factions, the fluctuations of popular allegiance and the uncertainties of war create constantly shifting situations to which the ruler must adapt himself as best he can.

The usual dramatic resource which Shakespeare employs to convey this kind of change is a messenger, or generally a series of messengers, bringing news of events to a character who is unaware of them. The messenger's sudden arrival, the unexpected nature of his news, the surprise with which it is received and his brief summary of events which may, in fact, have taken some time, all make the fact of change strike us more powerfully. Such is the effect of the arrival of news in Rome during the period of quiet after the banishment of Coriolanus. The city is apparently free from trouble, no longer threatened by invasion from the Volscians or by internal strife, following the banishment of Coriolanus, and the Tribunes survey the scene contentedly, congratulating themselves on their astuteness in getting rid of a trouble-maker:

> We hear not of him, neither need we fear him.
> His remedies are tame. The present peace
> And quietness of the people, which before
> Were in wild hurry, here do make his friends
> Blush that the world goes well; who rather had,
> Though they themselves did suffer by't, behold
> Dissentious numbers pest'ring streets than see
> Our tradesmen singing in their shops, and going
> About their functions friendly.
>   . . .
> The gods have well prevented it, and Rome
> Sits safe and still without him.   (IV vi 1–9; 36–7)

This peaceful domestic scene is interrupted by a messenger with news that the Volscians have entered Roman territory, an announcement which the Tribunes refuse to believe. He is quickly followed by a second messenger who declares that the senate is assembling and reports a rumour that Coriolanus is advancing on Rome at the head of a Volscian army, a notion which the Tribunes again dismiss as impossible. A third messenger then enters and confirms that the invasion has actually begun:

> A fearful army, led by Caius Marcius,
> Associated with Aufidius, rages

> Upon our territories, and have already
> O'erborne their way, consum'd with fire and took
> What lay before them.   (IV vi 76–80)

The section reaches its climax with the arrival of a fourth character, Cominius, accusing the Tribunes of causing the disaster:

> O, you have made good work!

By the end of the scene the Tribunes have reason to regret the action on which they earlier congratulated themselves and they leave the stage fearful and apprehensive at the change. Even though the audience knows before they do of Coriolanus's alliance with the Volscians, and therefore responds ironically to the Tribunes' expression of security, the gradual revelation of the news by a series of messengers makes us feel we are witnessing the process of change itself: the enemy seems to advance further at each revelation.

A similar effect occurs in the first scene of *Henry IV Part II* when news is brought to Northumberland in his castle in the north of events on the battlefield at Shrewsbury. Although this is an expository scene, Shakespeare has little information to convey – no more than that the rebels have been defeated and Hotspur has been killed. But he transforms what could have been an uneventful episode into one of great excitement and activity by distributing the news between three different messengers, two of whom arrive to contradict the first. Their confused reports recreate the uncertainty and doubtfulness of battle itself and we participate in Northumberland's fluctuations of mood from eagerness to grief and rage as he reacts to an apparently changing situation. One of the few characters in the histories who is largely untroubled by change is Richard III because, for most of the play, he is responsible for the deaths which constitute the shifts in power and has little need of messengers to tell him what he already knows. It is only towards the end of the fourth act (IV iv 433) that reports of events outside his control – the landing of Richmond, the gathering of enemy forces in the west and north – begin to arrive in quick succession (seven within a hundred lines of verse) and the appearance of these messengers is one of the signs we are given that Richard is losing his grip.

Some of the characters in the history plays attempt for a while to escape from the demands of politics, notably Antony in Alexandria

who, far from the centre of power in Rome, tries to ignore the continual changes which threaten the stability of the empire. He attempts to
prolong this illusion of freedom by refusing to hear the messengers
from Octavius, but his own 'Roman thought' gets the better of him
and, having heard of Fulvia's mutiny and Pompey's rebellion, he is
forced to submit to 'the strong necessity of time' and re-enter the
world of politics by leaving Alexandria. He has, in fact, never been out
of that world since his very presence in Egypt, like his later return
there, has political consequences. He leaves it only at his death, the
act which, as Cleopatra says, 'shackles accidents and bolts up
change'. Prince Hal, similarly, appears to abandon his obligations as
a prince by joining in the irresponsible life of the tavern at Eastcheap
where Hotspur and the King are subjects only for charades, but
though the company of Falstaff seems a perpetual holiday, we know
from the intervening scenes that the rebels are beginning to assemble,
and that the seclusion of tavern life is consequently threatened. The
major tavern scenes in both parts of *Henry IV* are interrupted by messengers summoning the Prince to his duties (II iv 278; II iv 342).
Moreover the irresponsibility which Hal and Falstaff seem to enjoy
together is partly a pretence: each in his way is using the other as a
means of achieving greater political power when Hal becomes King.
Each has a plan for the future of which their apparently spontaneous
association is a deliberately chosen part, and far from 'profaning the
precious time' they are, as they think, using it to their advantage. Like
Antony's association with Cleopatra, Hal's apparent profligacy has
political consequences but, unlike Antony's, it is carefully contrived.
The Boar's Head is as much affected by time as the world outside, and
when Hal walks out of the tavern and into the court at Westminster he
does not re-enter the world of politics because he has never actually
left it. All the characters in the history plays are 'time's subjects':[3]
even the hostess and Doll Tearsheet, the first victims of the law under
Hal's new regime, and in Rome a poet learns that it has become
dangerous to be called Cinna.

After his first defeat, Antony asks Octavius to let him retire as 'a
private man in Athens', and he is one of many Shakespearean characters who long to escape from politics. Richard II wants to be a beggar
or 'a mockery king of snow' that would melt away in the sunshine of
Bolingbroke, but he realises that even his imprisonment does not
exclude him from the world and that his 'sighs and tears and groans'
record the 'minutes, times and hours' of Bolingbroke's steady ascent

to power. Henry VI, weary of the chaos in a kingdom he is unable to control, longs for death. Dismissed as a nuisance to his own army, he withdraws from the battlefield at Towton, and his description of the violent, shifting fortunes of war suggests the continually changing political and military conflicts in which his life has been spent:

> Now sways it this way, like a mighty sea
> Forc'd by the tide to combat with the wind;
> Now sways it that way, like the selfsame sea
> Forc'd to retire by fury of the wind.
> Sometime the flood prevails, and then the wind;
> Now one the better, now another best;
> Both tugging to be victors, breast to breast.
>   (*3 Henry VI*, II v 5–11)

He envies what he imagines to be the life of a shepherd, not simply because it is free from 'care, mistrust and treason', but because it is predictable and easy to control. Time for the shepherd, he believes, brings a repeated, comforting pattern of changes:

> So many hours must I tend my flock;
> So many hours must I take my rest;
> So many hours must I contemplate;
> So many hours must I sport myself;
> So many days my ewes have been with young;
> So many weeks ere the poor fools will ean;
> So many years ere I shall shear the fleece:
> So minutes, hours, days, months and years
> Passed over to the end they were created,
> Would bring white hairs unto a quiet grave.   (II v 31–40)

These are like the regular, seasonal changes experienced by the shepherds in *The Winter's Tale* and *As You Like It*, not the random social upheavals of the history plays. In *Henry VI* the character whose life approaches nearest to the pastoral seclusion the king envies is Iden, the humble yeoman who, unlike Henry, is content with the inheritance he has received from his father. But even his retreat is invaded by the rebel Cade whom he is compelled to kill. In the following scene (*2 Henry VI*, v i 80) Iden receives as his reward the doubtful privilege of attending on the King and his seclusion is permanently finished.

Moreover, Henry's illusion that the common man is 'secure' is immediately dispelled by the entrance of two such 'poor harmless lambs', a son who has killed his father and a father who has killed his son. The former, it appears, was pressed into the King's army whereas his father was 'the Earl of Warwick's man' and therefore compelled to fight on the opposite side. They are not exempt from politics. Nor are the three ordinary citizens to whom Shakespeare devoted a masterly little scene in *Richard III*, a play mostly confined to the court. It is fear of change which disturbs them:

> 2 CITIZEN   Truly, the hearts of men are full of fear.
> You cannot reason almost with a man
> That looks not heavily and full of dread.
> 3 CITIZEN   Before the days of change, still it is so;
> By a divine instinct men's minds mistrust
> Ensuing danger.   (II iii 38–43)

The burdens which even Shakespeare's humblest characters are compelled to endure are, moreover, placed upon them as much by past as by present history, for the plays show the characters taking on problems created and handed on to them by their ancestors. They are born into political situations which are not of their own making and from which there is no escape. This idea is conveyed by the presentation of each individual history play as a fragment of a long, continuous, chronological sequence, an unbroken series of causes and effects. The frequent long speeches of historical summary or recapitulation, unique to these plays, serve to demonstrate that political actions have consequences far beyond their immediate present and that we are the subjects of past as well as present time. This is one reason for the appearance in *Henry VI Part I* of the aged Edmund Mortimer, a lonely survivor in prison of the rebellion, generations ago, against Henry IV.[4] Visited by his nephew, Richard, Mortimer treats him to an extensive history of the two previous reigns and an account of his genealogical descent from Edward III, from which it emerges that Richard should rightfully be king. The revelation encourages Richard's political ambitions and, once he has been made Duke of York, provides a motive for the rebellion which concludes with his torture and death in the *Third Part*, a disaster which in turn incites his sons to revenge, and leads to the murder of Henry VI and the establishment of Richard's son, Edward IV, on the throne. Mortimer's recital of past history, however undramatically written, is necessary to supply Richard with adequate motives for his ambitions, but at the same time it traces the causes of Henry VI's present troubles to the actions of Bolingbroke in seizing the throne and denying Mortimer his rights. By a continuous sequence of actions and reactions, all of them conceived by Shakespeare in human, psychological terms, the present is shown to be shaped by the past. Historical recollections of the kind given by Mortimer (and York tells the whole story again in the next play) are, incidentally, not peculiar to the English histories: *Julius Caesar* includes reminders of Pompey, an earlier victim of political assassination, whose death was a step in Caesar's progress towards supremacy, and the appearance of the ghost before the battle at Philippi reminds us that Brutus's death will occur as a natural consequence of Caesar's murder. But summaries of the distant past are much longer and more frequent in the English histories because these plays cover a far longer period and therefore allow Shakespeare to trace more elaborately the accumulating pressures of causes and effects. The ultimate first cause of the political troubles between the fall of Richard II and the accession of Henry Tudor is, of course, Bolingbroke's seizure of power, which is still being ruefully remembered in the reign of his grandson. Henry IV and his enemies are alike obsessed with their memory of his momentous landing at Ravenspurgh and never tire of recalling it, and his son, on the night before battle, reveals that he is still carrying the burden of his father's guilt. The characters in all these plays are haunted by the past because its effects continue to be felt through several generations.

The English histories are sometimes thought to depict a progress towards the happy reign of Queen Elizabeth, foretold at the end of *Henry VIII*. (See Tillyard's remark, quoted on p. 68 below.) No doubt Shakespeare was grateful for the freedom from civil war which she achieved and for the royal patronage enjoyed by his theatrical company, but he was too conscious of the precariousness of peace and the destructiveness of human nature to entertain any ideas of progress (a notion which, if we hold it at all today, we have inherited from the nineteenth century). The patterns of action in the history plays, however, portray a process of growth in the sense that the present is created by the past. This weight of the past is often very powerfully conveyed in the way a history play actually begins. In the first moments of *Henry VI Part I* the peers are already feeling the effects of the death of Henry V as they kneel round his coffin; their petty quarrels show that their private intrigues have been held back only by the King's strong personality and that, now he is dead, the unity of the court is disintegrating. We shortly discover that, in the hands of a dissentious court, the empire in France they have inherited from Henry V becomes a liability. Presumably Shakespeare learned how to plunge *in medias res* from his reading of classical epic and the rules derived from it, and such openings certainly arouse the interest of an audience, but their effect is not simply theatrical. The first line of the *Third Part*,

> I wonder how the King escap'd our hands,

thrusts us even more rapidly into the action, and conveys more strongly than any of the other histories the feeling that the play never really had a beginning. *Henry IV* opens with the King's cry of weariness at the prolonged anxieties of a civil war for which he is not wholly responsible, and Shakespeare makes an immediate, ironic contrast between this care-worn man and the self-possessed Bolingbroke of the previous play who adroitly accepted the power which has now become a burden to him.

Even the first play chronologically, *Richard II*, opens in the middle of a feud caused by a murder already committed, and contains frequent references back to Edward III, the ancestor of all the major characters, by the standard of whose exemplary government Richard's ineptitude is measured. *Troilus and Cressida* also begins, as the Prologue tells us 'in the middle', with the Trojan War still continuing seven years after the abduction of Helen, the event which started it. By the end of the play, Hector has been slaughtered, Troilus has won and lost Cressida, the generals have debated to no effect and the war still goes on. The play shows a portion of a process which has neither beginning nor end. Shakespeare perceives that no successor to the throne is given a fresh start: a ruler must cope with the problems left to him by his ancestors and, when he dies, he hands on different problems to his heirs. Thus the last moments of the plays initiate new actions as the first moments show a continuation of old actions. Within the five acts of a history play we are made conscious of Act Minus I and Act VI. Though Richard II dies, his play actually ends with Bolingbroke's remorse at the murder and his resolutions to make a pilgrimage of repentance:

Come, mourn with me for what I do lament,
And put on sullen black incontinent.
I'll make a voyage to the Holy Land
To wash this blood off from my guilty hand.   (v vi 47–50)

The last act of *Henry V* is largely devoted to a proposal of marriage and a peace conference, but it is followed by an epilogue to remind us that the King's reign was very brief and that his son failed to keep the empire in France which we have watched Henry struggle to conquer. The general construction of the first tetralogy is obviously designed to represent Shakespeare's sense of the continuous process of history, since the tragic episodes, the deaths of Talbot, Humphrey of Gloucester, York, Warwick and Henry VI occur anywhere except at the conclusion of a play and hence the endings have none of the finality associated with the death of a tragic hero. What we do see in the closing scenes is the beginning of the action of the play which follows. The *First Part* ends with the arrangement of the royal marriage which then takes place in the *Second Part*; this play ends with young Clifford's resolution to avenge his father's death and York's decision to pursue the King, both of which reach their outcome in the *Third Part*; this in turn concludes with the spurious tranquillity of Edward IV's accession and the concealed ambitions of Richard of Gloucester with which *Richard III* begins. A feature of each play, as Geoffrey Bullough points out,[5] is 'the emergence towards the end of one major character who will be important in the next': Suffolk in the *First Part*, York in the *Second Part* and Richard of Gloucester in the *Third Part*. A similar process takes place towards the end of *Richard II* with the first appearance of Hotspur and the references to Prince Hal's profligacy. The end of *Richard III*, of course, sees the emergence of Richmond and there is no theoretical reason why Shakespeare should not have continued to write history plays portraying English affairs up to the moment at which he was actually writing, thereby creating the kind of problems which worried Tristram Shandy. *Richard III* concludes with a prayer:

Abate the edge of traitors, gracious Lord,
That would reduce these bloody days again   (v v 35–6)

and no doubt Richmond speaks for Shakespeare's audience who knew that there had been work for the executioners since Richmond's accession. Even the apparently conclusive ending of *Henry VIII*, in

Northrop Frye's opinion, is not untroubled since it portrays 'the triumph of Cranmer, Cromwell and Anne Boleyn, along with the audience's knowledge of what soon happened to them'.[6] The character who 'emerges' – literally – at the end of that play is, of course, the infant Elizabeth and the first audiences to see her knew that her reign was not without problems passed on by her predecessors.

Shakespeare's portrayal of history as an endless process is one aspect of his depiction of the 'temporal life'. This picture arouses our pity because it shows men trying to assert their individuality in a world where their freedom of action is curtailed by the dead as well as the living. Moreover the idealism of a Brutus or a Hector, the ambitions of a York or a Richard of Gloucester, and even the famous victories of Henry V are made to seem small and temporary in the context of history. 'If you consider the infinite extent of eternity', says Boethius, 'what satisfaction can you have about the power of your name to endure?'[7]

This double vision appears at its most powerful in *Troilus and Cressida*, the play set furthest from Shakespeare's own day. Through the characters we are induced to visualise the Trojan War in the context of a global history which will eventually obliterate all recollection of them:

> What's past and what's to come is strew'd with husks
> And formless ruin of oblivion.   (IV v 166–7)

Agamemnon here expresses the sense, felt by practically all the major characters, of the irresistible effects of time and change. Nevertheless he clings to the necessary ideals of fidelity and truth even as he feels them evaporate:

> But in this extant moment, faith and troth,
> Strain'd purely from all hollow bias-drawing,
> Bids thee with most divine integrity,
> From heart of very heart, great Hector, welcome.
> (ibid., 168–71)

It is towards similar permanent ideals that Troilus and Cressida themselves aspire in their pledges of fidelity, resolving that, in spite of 'sad mortality', their love will survive (a resolution which itself shortly proves vulnerable to the effects of time):

> When time is old and hath forgot itself,
> When waterdrops have worn the stones of Troy,
> And blind oblivion swallow'd cities up,
> And mighty states characterless are grated
> To dusty nothing – yet let memory
> From false to false, among false maids in love,
> Upbraid my falsehood.   (III ii 181–7)

This is, again, a double vision which includes both Cressida's terrifying feeling of being obliterated and our knowledge that she will be remembered – though, by a further irony, for the one fault she swore not to commit.

This awareness of the temporary nature of human achievement is not confined simply to the dramatist and his audience. It is felt by the older characters such as Nestor, the 'good old chronicle' who has 'walked hand in hand with time'. The longevity of such people allows them to look back on the rise and fall of princes or to complain that the achievements of the fathers are destroyed by their children. They supply tragic complaints of the 'Was it for this?' variety. Duke Humphrey, the surviving brother of Henry V, lives to see Henry VI's improvident marriage to Margaret of Anjou and the casual abandonment of the territories in France:

> What! did my brother Henry spend his youth,
> His valour, coin, and people in the wars?
> Did he so often lodge in open field,
> In winter's cold and summer's parching heat,
> To conquer France, his true inheritance?
> . . .
> O peers of England, shameful is this league!
> Fatal this marriage, cancelling your fame,
> Blotting your names from books of memory,
> Razing the characters of your renown,
> Defacing monuments of conquer'd France,
> Undoing all, as all had never been!
>   (*2 Henry VI,* I i 73–7; 93–8)

The surviving descendants of Edward III – Gaunt, York and Gloucester's widow – look with dismay at the treachery of his grandson and the decay of the kingdom. Three survivors from the past haunt the court of Richard III: the widow of York (a former aspirant to the throne); Queen Elizabeth, the widow of Edward IV; and the aged Queen Margaret, widow of Henry VI, whom Shakespeare unhistorically brings back to England as a reminder of the uncertainties of fortune. Together they join in an antiphonal and 'woe-wearied' complaint against the monotonously bloody pattern of murder and revenge which has constituted the history of the last three reigns. But the most moving expression of the bewildering fluctuations of history is given to Henry IV towards the end of his life when he views with incomprehension the formation and breaking of factions he has seen. His own experience leads him to see the process of time as essentially one of dispiriting and bewildering change which, if we could foresee it, would make us unwilling to live:

> O God! That one might read the book of fate
> And see the revolution of the times
> Make mountains level, and the continent,
> Weary of solid firmness, melt itself
> Into the sea; and other times to see
> The beachy girdle of the ocean
> Too wide for Neptune's hips; how chances mock
> And changes fill the cup of alteration
> With divers liquors! O, if this were seen,
> The happiest youth, viewing his progress through,
> What perils past, what crosses to ensue,
> Would shut the book, and sit him down and die.
>
> (III i 45–56)

Henry IV does live, however, to see the end of the Percys' rebellion which his own rise to power had provoked, but by one of the ironies of history which Shakespeare was quick to appreciate, he hears of his victory only when he is on the verge of death and already too infirm to enjoy it. This irony compels from him the bitter complaint,

> Will Fortune never come with both hands full?

Having survived the shocks of continual political change, Henry finds himself destroyed by the resistless process of age. As I have shown, other history plays contain individual characters who have been allowed the doubtful privilege of surviving beyond their contemporaries, and who live on to see the ruin of what they have created, but, as Robert Ornstein remarks, 'only in the second tetralogy do men actually grow old, and only in *Henry IV Part II* is there the poignancy of age with its attendant loss of vitality, optimism and personal ties'.[8] This is everywhere so apparent – in the King's weariness and isolation, in Lady Percy's lament for the loss of Hotspur, Shallow's reflections on the death of his 'old acquaintance' and, above all, in the decline of Falstaff – that it needs little comment. It is also achieved by the subtle changes which Shakespeare has made to the characters who survive from the *First Part*, and the loss of those who gave to the *First Part* its characteristic variety and energy. The rebellion in the *First Part*, motivated largely by grudges against Henry by those who helped him to power, was at least given a certain style, zest and idealism by the presence of Hotspur. In the *Second Part* he is mentioned only to be mourned. The tavern scenes in the *First Part* are animated by Falstaff's wit and his association with Prince Hal: their exchanges of insult and contests of wit are so fluent that they seem to be the result of long familiarity. But in the *Second Part* Hotspur is replaced by the high-minded but muddle-headed Archbishop Scroop, and Hal and Falstaff meet only once before the final rejection. In his first scene Falstaff has no audience but his page and the Lord Chief Justice. His monstrous lies are delivered into vacancy. There is no need for Shakespeare to tell us that these characters are in decline: their behaviour shows it. When they do complain of the effects of time they do so in the language of people who are feeling it in particular, identifiable ways.

Although Shakespeare can make powerful, aphoristic generalisations about time, in the King's soliloquies and in the Sonnets, he also knows that it shows its effects in Falstaff's urine and Shallow's rambling conversation. Falstaff's tangible decline has already begun in the *First Part*:

> Bardolph, am I not fall'n away vilely since this last action? Do I not bate? Do I not dwindle? Why, my skin hangs about me like an old lady's loose gown; I am withered like an old apple-john.
>
> (*1 Henry IV*, iii iii 1–6)

His defiant claim to set his name in 'the scroll of youth' carries no weight with the Lord Chief Justice, who enumerates the signs of Falstaff's decay with ruthless particularity

Have you not a moist eye, a dry hand, a yellow cheek, a white beard, a decreasing leg, an increasing belly? Is not your voice broken, your wind short, your chin double, your wit single, and every part about you blasted with antiquity?

(*2 Henry IV*, ɪ ii 168–74)

Falstaff cannot always sustain the illusion that he is young. His protestations of youthfulness are partly an 'act' to amuse his listeners, and in a maudlin interlude with Doll Tearsheet, beautifully achieved by Shakespeare, he admits 'I am old'. What he fails to recognise is that the times have changed and that Henry V is no longer his apparently close companion from Eastcheap. For him, as for the King, good news comes too late. Overtaken both by the tide of events and by his own decay, he has, it seems, no alternative but to die. It is odd that Shakespeare could have thought to 'continue the story, with Sir John in it'. The story, of course, does continue, but his absence is telling: he has become a casualty of history.

The changes in an individual are not always the result of physical and mental decay: Shakespeare sometimes portrays developments within a personality brought about by new experiences. The developments in Bolingbroke's personality from his first appearance in *Richard II* to his dying moments in *Henry IV Part II* are sufficiently steady and consistent to be credible, and an actor would have little difficulty in making his performance convincing if he were to act the role in all three plays in succession. Yet nobody would argue that the self-confident administrator of the first play is the 'same man' as the anguished solitary of the last, any more than the Othello of the final act of his tragedy is the same as the one of the first. This truism would not be worth mentioning were it not for the fact that such changes sometimes strike Shakespeare's characters with the force of a new and horrifying discovery – and, indeed, we might conjecture that, had Bolingbroke actually been able to 'look into the book of fate', he would have chosen not to develop into Henry IV. It seems incredible to Hamlet that his father's wife could have become the wife of Claudius, and Troilus is so appalled by the change in Cressida from the constant mistress to the coquette of the Greek camp that he is unable to reconcile the two:

This she? No; this is Diomed's Cressida.
If beauty have a soul, this is not she;

> If souls guide vows, if vows be sanctimonies,
> If sanctimony be the gods' delight,
> If there be rule in unity itself,
> This was not she. O madness of discourse,
> That cause sets up with and against itself!   (v ii 135–41)

We may well feel that Cressida has not actually changed and that his earlier opinion of her was simply mistaken, but in that case we must conclude that the very quality of Cressida's character which Troilus failed to perceive was her changeableness and it is this which has such a profound effect on him.

The changes of character or policy or mood by men in power can, in turn, affect the lives of their favourites, as Shakespeare must have observed in the careers of noblemen like Raleigh and Essex. 'The followers of men in power', says Boethius, 'can be destroyed by the fall of their leader, or even by his whim when he is still in power.'[9] Buckingham, as his career reaches its summit, suddenly loses the favour of Richard III and is denied the earldom promised to him because the King is 'not in the giving vein', and he tries to escape with his life. Humphrey of Gloucester, a victim of court intrigue, is accused of treason and murdered in his bed. The most memorable victim of a king's apparent change of mind is, of course, Falstaff, also rejected at what he imagines is the moment of his arrival in power. Wolsey, the most powerful man in England, is destroyed by the envious faction at the court and discovers the precariousness of those who 'hang on princes' favours'. Another victim of this kind, Hastings, vividly describes his sense of precipitate change when the King turns against him:

> Who builds his hope in air of your good looks
> Lives like a drunken sailor on a mast,
> Ready with every nod to tumble down
> Into the fatal bowels of the deep.   (*Richard III*, iii iv 100–3)

The most profound difference between Eden and the 'vita temporalis' to which Adam was banished was, of course, the advent of death, the final change in a human life which is never still: the larger history of nations contains the personal tragedies of the people who contribute to it. Yet the effect even of this most solitary experience is not confined to the individual: the deaths of powerful men like Richard II, Henry V and Julius Caesar create changes in society, making even their most private act a political one. Some of them see death approaching and, in their last moments, have the opportunity to take account of their lives. In these crises characters like Warwick and Henry IV experience a combination of a 'reversal of fortune' and a 'discovery' which Aristotle identified as characteristic of tragedy. Their fortune changes from prosperity to imminent non-existence, like that of the exemplary figures in the *Mirror for Magistrates*, a source of several of the history plays, and, like the characters in the *Mirror*, they discover the worthlessness of those achievements from which death separates them:

> These eyes, that now are dimm'd with death's black veil,
> Have been as piercing as the mid-day sun
> To search the secret treasons of the world;
> The wrinkles in my brows, now filled with blood,
> Were lik'ned oft to kingly sepulchres;
> For who liv'd King, but I could dig his grave?
> And who durst smile when Warwick bent his brow?
> Lo now my glory smear'd in dust and blood!
> My parks, my walks, my manors, that I had,
> Even now forsake me; and of all my lands
> Is nothing left me but my body's length.
> Why, what is pomp, rule, reign, but earth and dust?
>
> (*3 Henry VI*, v ii 16–28)

Warwick the Kingmaker's tragic discovery is similar to Richard II's helpless realisation that he must exchange his 'large kingdom' for a 'little grave'. One of the most moving statements of the contrast between the greatness of human achievement and its annihilation by death is given to Mark Antony as he meditates over the body of Julius Caesar:

> O mighty Caesar! Dost thou lie so low?
> Are all thy conquests, glories, triumphs, spoils,
> Shrunk to this little measure? Fare thee well.   (iii i 149–51)

Death in Shakespeare's history plays is the final transformation his characters undergo in a world which is governed by time.

The two best-known proverbs describing time contradict each other: time is said to be a great healer but it is also said to consume all things. The healing effects of time appear in the comedies where couples meet, woo and wed, or families are separated and united as the year moves on from winter to spring, but time in the history plays, like time in the Sonnets, is the destroyer of rocks impregnable and gates of steel, *tempus edax rerum* whose pervasive effects are described in the last book of Ovid's *Metamorphoses*. Many of Shakespeare's historical characters are driven by the appetite for power, but once in power they seek to establish an unshakeable structure which will resist the effects of time: Humphrey of Gloucester struggles to control rival political factions, Richard III to destroy his competitors, Henry IV to create a stable society, Henry V a united and powerful nation, Brutus a government founded on 'peace, freedom and liberty', Ulysses an ordered and united military machine, Octavius a stable triumvirate cemented by Antony's marriage to Octavia. Their desire, like Macbeth's, is to be 'perfect, whole as the marble, founded as the rock'. They fail because the edifices they try to build are human and therefore subject to the effects of time. Shakespeare expresses a similar anxiety about the transience of all earthly things in the Sonnets, but there it is counterbalanced by a faith in the enduring power of love. Love has only a very small part to play in the history plays, however, where marriages are made for political reasons and women like Brutus's wife or Lady Percy are not much more than adjuncts in the careers of their husbands. The love of Troilus and Cressida is portrayed in order that it may be shown to be ephemeral and the love of Antony and Cleopatra, constantly threatened by the instability of the protagonists and the world they live in, can survive only in a dimension outside time.

Shakespeare portrays history as a series of attempts by individuals to satisfy their need for permanence, and their necessary failure to create it. The vigour, intelligence and optimism of men like Richard III, Henry V and Antony are heroic because they are applied to a struggle not simply against temporal human beings but against time itself. This is one of the reasons why the effect of the history plays is often tragic: history, for Shakespeare, consists of a series of heroic and unequal struggles to defeat the power of time.

3 | *Fortune and Nature*

Some of the effects of time discussed in the last chapter are predictable: the changing seasons and the seven ages of man are part of a familiar, repeated pattern of existence. But the transformations which states and societies undergo, especially the fluctuations of war and the rise and fall of princes, seem to happen quite arbitrarily, and when they occur their victims naturally attempt to find a cause for them. Shakespeare's characters ascribe such events, depending on their beliefs, either to divine providence or to fortune or to the actions of men. The history plays are, in part, an analysis of the causes of social and political crisis, and the analysis begins in the first lines of the *First Part of Henry VI*.

The play begins in the aftermath of a political catastrophe, the premature and sudden death of Henry V; and in the opening dialogue his peers, as they stand round his coffin, speculate whether the king was the victim of 'inauspicious stars' or the malevolence of his enemies. Bedford attributes the tragedy to 'the bad revolting stars' or 'adverse planets in the heavens', whereas Exeter prefers to blame the 'subtle-witted French' whose sorcerers have destroyed him by magic spells. This conversation has in it the makings of a debate on the relative power of fortune and man to control human affairs, a subject which had interested philosophers and historians since classical times[1] and continued to occupy the minds of Shakespeare and his contemporaries. Arguments about the respectability of astrology as a science were part of this larger debate and these went on until well after the foundation of the Royal Society.[2] Plutarch, in Holland's translation, declares that 'all things roll and run at a venture, and . . . there is no other cause of good and evil accidents of this life, but either fortune or else the will of man'[3]. Machiavelli admits that many have been and are of the opinion that human affairs are so governed by Fortune and by God, that men cannot alter them by any prudence of theirs, and indeed have no remedy against them; and for this reason have come to think that it is not worth while to labour much about anything, but that they must leave everything to be determined by chance.[4]

Machiavelli sympathises with this passive acceptance of events, particularly in view of 'the great changes in things which we have seen, and every day see happen contrary to human expectation', but the strong emphasis of his political writings is on the power of the individual to control the otherwise random course of history.

Like time, fortune was thought to have made its entrance into the world as a consequence of the fall of man. Hence Boccaccio begins his survey of the tragedies of great men who have fallen victims to fortune, the *De Casibus Virorum Illustrium*, with an account of the fall of Adam, which 'made possible the later falls of princes'.[5] Before their expulsion from Eden, Adam and Eve had led unchanging lives in which their desires coincided with the will of God in a harmonious world, but their disobedience introduced violently conflicting elements into nature and left them exposed to the operation of chance. Lydgate, in his enlargement of Boccaccio's gloomy narratives, states the notion clearly:

> Thus cam in first thoruh inobedience,
> As bi a gate, pouerte and neede;
> And at ther bak folwed indigence,
> Sorwe, siknesse, maladie and dreede,
> Exil, banshyng and seruitute, in deede,
> Which causid man longe to contune
> Vndir the lordshipe & daunger off Fortune.[6]

Milton, in the tenth book of *Paradise Lost*, describes the deterioration which occurs in the physical world as a consequence of the fall of Adam and Eve: the climate, hitherto calm and temperate, now turns tempestuous and brings painful extremes of heat and cold; the creatures, formerly at peace, begin to prey on one another, and man, no longer destined to a predictable future, becomes subject to the 'noxious efficacy' of the planets.[7]

Fortune and its agents the stars are often held responsible by

Shakespeare's characters for their otherwise inexplicable failures and successes in war, as when the Dauphin remarks that the planet Mars has transferred its influence from the English army to the French:

> Mars his true moving, even as in the heavens
> So in the earth, to this day is not known.
> Late did he shine upon the English side;
> Now we are victors, upon us he smiles.
> What towns of any moment but we have?
> At pleasure here we lie near Orleans;
> Otherwhiles the famish'd English, like pale ghosts,
> Faintly besiege us one hour in a month.   (*1 Henry VI*, i ii 1–8)

Henry VI, helplessly observing the fall of Duke Humphrey of Gloucester at the hands of the Queen and her faction, enquires why such a harmless, innocent man can have become so hated:

> What louring star now envies thy estate
> That these great lords, and Margaret our Queen,
> Do seek subversion of thy harmless life?   (*2 Henry VI*, iii i 206–8)

Richard II's queen, just after his departure for Ireland, senses that 'some unborn sorrow, ripe in fortune's womb' is advancing upon her (ii ii 9–13), a premonition which is immediately confirmed. This idea – that men are the helpless victims of the planets – is stated as an axiom by the Duke in *Measure for Measure* in his account of the human condition generally:

> A breath thou art,
> Servile to all the skyey influences,
> That dost this habitation where thou keep'st
> Hourly afflict.   (iii i 8–11)

The evidence shows, therefore, that Shakespeare's characters tend to attribute to fortune those changes in events which are not caused by any apparent human agency. Whether Shakespeare himself shared their belief is, however, another matter. His outlook seems in many ways so much like our own that we are disinclined to think of a Shakespeare who believed in astrology. Certainly some of his most intelligent and learned contemporaries, such as the mathematician John

Dee, were practising astrologers (it was Dee who advised Queen Elizabeth on the most auspicious date for her coronation), and Shakespeare was well acquainted with their theories and terms of art.

It may be useful if we here make a distinction (though Shakespeare himself was not so systematic) between three different kinds of effect which fortune and the stars have been thought to produce on man. The first is the astrological influence on human character and temperament brought about by the particular conjunction of the stars at the moment of a man's birth, an effect which professional astrologers claimed they could calculate by drawing up what was technically known as a 'nativity' or horoscope. The second is what we should now describe as 'chance' or 'luck', the brief, unexpected and otherwise unaccountable turn of events for better or for worse. The third is a more extended, long-term process which may show itself during a complex series of actions involving many people, as in the course of an entire play, to which we shall give the name of 'destiny' or 'fate'. All three notions imply that men are not wholly in control of their actions, that their powers are circumscribed.

Such teleological questions are asked most frequently and urgently in *King Lear*, the play in which men behave most unfeelingly and in ways which appear inhuman by conventional standards. Some of the characters in this play (Lear, Gloucester, Kent, Albany), rejecting as inadequate any 'natural' explanation for the barbarities which are committed, attribute them to the influence on man of the supernatural. There is, as Bradley says, 'in most of the better characters a preoccupation with the question of the ultimate power, and a passionate need to explain by reference to it what otherwise would drive them to despair'.[8] The precise nature and motives of this 'ultimate power' remain, however, beyond their comprehension and different characters conceive of it in different, conflicting ways, leaving an audience uncertain as to its true identity and purpose. Kent attributes the differences in personality between Cordelia and her sisters to astrological influences, and Gloucester also believes that the social disintegrations which take place in the opening scenes are brought about by the stars:

These late eclipses in the sun and moon portend no good to us. Though the wisdom of nature can reason it thus and thus, yet nature finds itself scourg'd by the sequent effects: love cools, friendship falls off, brothers divide; in cities, mutinies; in countries, discord; in palaces, treason; and the bond crack'd 'twixt son and father. (ɪ ii 100–8)

Immediately after these words, however, Edmund describes his father's notions as merely superstitious:

> This is the excellent foppery of the world, that, when we are sick in fortune, often the surfeits of our own behaviour, we make guilty of our disasters the sun, the moon, and stars; as if we were villains on necessity; fools by heavenly compulsion; knaves, thieves and treachers, by spherical predominance; drunkards, liars and adulterers, by an enforc'd obedience of planetary influence; and all that we are evil in, by a divine thrusting on – an admirable evasion of whoremaster man, to lay his goatish disposition on the charge of a star! (ɪ ii 117–27)

The two opinions are, needless to say, in complete opposition. Whether Shakespeare himself believed that character was determined by astrological influence we have no means of knowing. He would be unlikely to agree with Edmund, who is the more ruthlessly cynical of the two characters, but Gloucester is at the same time credulous and easily deceived. Taken as a whole, the play gives confirmation to neither point of view: the 'ultimate power' remains unknowable.

Elsewhere Shakespeare refers frequently to the distinction between the 'gifts of fortune' and those of 'nature' in determining a person's character and station in life, a distinction which, as H. R. Patch has shown, had a long literary history.[9] The difference is roughly one between the attributes bestowed on a person by circumstances, such as social position, wealth and worldly possessions, and the innate qualities with which he is born, such as strength, beauty and intelligence. As Rosalind points out during a little debate on the subject in *As You Like It*, 'Fortune reigns in the gifts of the world, not in the lineaments of Nature' (ɪ ii 37–9),[10] and as Hamlet says, a defect may be the result of 'nature's livery or fortune's star' (ɪ iv 32). But although Shakespeare's characters regularly make a distinction between these two influences, his plays indicate, as we shall see, that they are not so easily separated. Even this theory, moreover, implies that human action is confined by forces beyond our control.

Shakespeare's private beliefs are inaccessible to us: all we can know are the opinions of his characters and these, as we have seen, differ widely. In any case our concern is to elucidate the effects of his plays and these may or may not be consistent with any personal opinion he may have held. There is, however, no doubt that fortune in the second sense, that of 'chance' or 'luck', plays a significant role in the action of the history plays, particularly in war and in the earliest of the histories where war forms a major and almost continuous part of the action. Shakespeare's principal source for the *Henry VI* plays, Hall's chronicle, itself contained repeated examples of the ironies of fortune and melancholy reflections by the chronicler on the helplessness and ignorance of man, as in his closing remark on the decapitation of York by Clifford:

[He] caused his head to be stryken of, and set on it a croune of paper, & so fixed it on a pole, & presented it to the Quene . . . saiying: Madame, your warre is done, here is your kinges raunsome, at which present, was much ioy, and great reioysing, but many laughed then, that sore lamented after, as the Quene her self, and her sonne: And many were glad then of other mens deaths, not knowing that their awne were nere at hande, as the Lord Clifford and other. But surely mans nature is so frayle, that thinges passed be sone forgotten, and mischiefes to come, be not forsene.[11]

The ironical tone of this last sentence is close to that in which the early history plays were written: Shakespeare discovered in Hall's chronicle a very congenial source.

Comparison between Hall's and Shakespeare's version of the same episodes reveals that the dramatist made radical changes to his source in order to increase the role of fortune in the sense of 'chance', to emphasise its ironies, and even to create such ironies where they had not previously existed. His reconstruction from Hall of the circumstances leading to the death of Salisbury is characteristic. In the chronicle we are first told that there was a tower just outside the walls of Orleans, in the top of which was a room from where the English generals used to spy into the town. The French, Hall goes on, discovered this 'totyng hole' and directed a cannon towards it. Salisbury, with the other leaders, happened to go up into the room but was spotted by a boy, the son of the French master gunner, who

toke his matche, as his father had taught hym, whiche was gone doune to dinner, and fired the gonne, whiche brake & shevered the

yron barres of the grate, whereof one strake therle so strongly on the
hed, that it stroke away one of his iyes and the side of his cheke.[12]

The Earl dies several days later. Hall's account is obviously not without its ironies, and he does attribute Salisbury's death to chance, but
Shakespeare's adaptation of Hall's narrative when he wrote the scene
for *Henry VI Part I*, particularly his alteration of the order of events,
emphasises the fortuitous nature of the affair, the unwarranted com-
placency of the victims and the irony of Salisbury's destruction by a
mere child. At the beginning of the scene (I iv) we see the gunner's son
complaining to his father that, though he has often taken shots at the
English soldiers, he has never actually hit one. His father assures the
boy that he is about to have better luck because he has pointed a
cannon directly at the tower where the English come to peer into the
city. The gunner then goes off, leaving his son in charge of the cannon.
The trap is thus prepared in advance. Salisbury, Talbot and their
aides then appear on the tower with the ominously explicit words,

> Discourse, I prithee, on this turret's top.

The audience, waiting no doubt for the other necessary participant in
the catastrophe, is gratified by the stealthy entrance of the boy 'with a
linstock'. In conversation, Salisbury promises to avenge on the French
the insults with which they have injured Talbot, and 'seeing it is
supper-time in Orleans', he invites his colleagues to peer through the
grating and consider where best to mount their attack:

> Let us look in; the sight will much delight thee.

The boy promptly fires his father's cannon instantly killing both
Salisbury and Gargrave. Talbot, not knowing who has fired the gun,
compounds the irony by cursing the hand that has destroyed them:

> Accursed tower! accursed fatal hand
> That hath contriv'd this woeful tragedy!
> In thirteen battles Salisbury o'ercame;
> Henry the Fifth he first train'd to the wars;
> Whilst any trump did sound or drum struck up,
> His sword did ne'er leave striking in the field. (I iv 76–81)

Only the spectator knows how fortuitously the tragedy has occurred and he is placed in the position of an all-seeing fortune with which he is forced to be tacitly implicated. Shakespeare's verse does not make for tragic seriousness, but its woodenness may here be deliberate: Talbot's expression of grief is like that of an automaton responding mechanically to a blow for which fortune has set him up.

The early histories abound in ironies of this simple kind: Joan the Pucelle, who claims to be assigned by God to be 'the English scourge', is praised extravagantly by the Dauphin after her initial victory:

> Divinest creature, Astræa's daughter,
> How shall I honour thee for this success?
> Thy promises are like Adonis' gardens,
> That one day bloom'd and fruitful were the next.
>
> (*1 Henry VI*, i vi 4–7)

She is defeated in the next scene and her soldiers appear jumping ignominiously from the walls of Orleans in their nightshirts, an ironic sequence of events created by Shakespeare's redeployment of Hall's material. The effect depends primarily on the order in which the dramatist chose to portray events. Irving Ribner is, of course, correct when he remarks that there is 'little attempt at chronological consistency' in these early plays and that 'the order of events is often confused',[13] but needless to say Shakespeare does not portray history accurately; he creates those 'probable' or 'necessary' sequences of events which, according to Aristotle, make tragedy more 'philosophical' than history. Shakespeare's version of history at this early stage in his career places a greater stress on the power of fortune than does Hall's. The result is obviously to increase the theatrical effect of the narrative by engaging the audience's attention in its ironies. But theatrical effects seldom, if ever, exist without creating further implications which are not exclusively dramatic. Shakespeare's greater emphasis on the supernatural agency of fortune tends to reduce the stature of his characters, to show that their scope for action is seriously limited and to place the audience, with its superior access to information, in the position of a fortune which, nevertheless, it is unable to control. We experience a feeling of intent and excited frustration and may even wish to jump onto the stage and warn the unsuspecting victims, a form of audience participation not uncommon at performances of *Othello*, but our well-meaning intervention would be useless since it would merely transform the characters into the actors who play their roles. Our only expedient would be to leave the theatre and allow events to take their course.

As Plutarch observed, however, the other cause of 'good or evil accidents' is the will of man and in the *Henry VI* plays disasters are more often the result of human fallibility than of chance. The King's ineptitude, the irresponsible feuds of the nobility, and the ambitions of various political adventurers are also the cause of the country's ruin. As he developed, Shakespeare took an increasing interest in the psychological origins of political change and paid much greater attention to creating full and complex characters in plays which depend less on the simple interventions of fortune, and replace physical action with more static situations in which characters have time to reveal themselves at leisure. The change of emphasis is obvious in *Richard II* which has no battle scenes but many lyrical passages of verse in which the King's complex character unfolds itself. The struggle, such as it is, between Bolingbroke and Richard is, to put it crudely, one between a man who knows how to manage his affairs and one who does not. Even as he goes into exile, Bolingbroke takes care to ingratiate himself with the common people at a time when Richard is losing their favour. Moreover Bolingbroke is given the support of the nobility because they are weary of Richard's ineptitude, so that by the time he sets foot again in England, Bolingbroke is met 'in boroughs, cities, villages', attended on bridges and in lanes (*1 Henry IV*, iv iii 69–70) by loyal supporters, and finds virtually the whole country behind him. The 'opinion', as he later describes it, which helped him to the crown, is won by his own exertions and Richard's negligence, and Richard is left with nothing but the 'small model of the barren earth' he stands up in. The final step, the actual transfer of power, takes place entirely as a consequence of the conflicting personalities of the two men and has the inevitability of a chemical reaction:

> Methinks King Richard and myself should meet
> With no less terror than the elements
> Of fire and water, when their thund'ring shock
> At meeting tears the cloudy cheeks of heaven.   (iii iii 54–7)

Contrary to Bolingbroke's expectations, however, it is not himself but Richard who provides the watery element: it is in Richard's nature to submit without even being asked to do so:

> What must the King do now? Must he submit?
> The King shall do it. Must he be depos'd?
> The King shall be contented.   (III iii 143–5)

As Robert Ornstein puts it, Bolingbroke 'need not scale the forbidden heights of power, because Richard descends to his own abasement'.[14] The tragedy issues entirely from the effects on each other of the characters of the two men. It is not simply that, in the familiar expression, Richard's character is his fate, but that the interactions between these two unique individuals determine their fates. To that extent *Richard II* creates an impression of fortune operating in a more prolonged, indirect and complex way than it did on the tower outside Orleans. It assumes the third of its functions mentioned earlier in this chapter, that of destiny.

The sense of fortune in its role of destiny is continously transmitted to an audience during the process which leads to the assassination of Julius Caesar. As Shakespeare portrays it, the murder is conceived, plotted and successfully accomplished entirely as a result of the reactions on one another of certain unique individuals, particularly Cassius, Brutus and Caesar himself; the specific combination of these characters leads, in a way which is made to appear inevitable, to disaster. The dynamic force which starts the conspiracy is provided by Cassius. He is powerfully driven by a combination of motives: envy, political idealism, whether genuine or feigned for the benefit of Brutus, and an expressed conviction that Caesar is already a tyrant. He also realises that he needs the support of Brutus if he is to succeed and has a sufficiently shrewd understanding of Brutus to be able to manipulate him. For his part, Brutus is unable to see that he is being manipulated and responds to precisely those principles of honour and political conscience to which Cassius appeals:

> BRUTUS   If it be aught toward the general good,
> Set honour in one eye and death i'th' other,
> And I will look on both indifferently;
> For let the gods so speed me as I love
> The name of honour more than I fear death.
> CASSIUS   I know that virtue to be in you, Brutus,
> As well as I do know your outward favour.
> Well, honour is the subject of my story.   (I ii 85–92)

Brutus's reputation as a man of honour is sufficient to give the conspiracy the appearance of respectability that Cassius knows it needs, and other patricians are content to support it merely because it has the seal of Brutus's approval: Caius Ligarius follows simply because Brutus leads. Once Cassius has acquired the support of the other conspirators, they in turn require the co-operation of their victim: Caesar must be persuaded into a position where he can be destroyed. But Caesar is temperamentally so easily flattered and so blind to the conspiracy that he allows his 'good friends' to conduct him to the Capitol in order that he may receive the daggers which they have prepared for him. The first three acts of *Julius Caesar* are a wonderfully constructed dramatic machine which, in order to work, requires each human part to perform its necessary function.

Each character does fulfill his function (as we know he will) because, apparently, he chooses to do so. Yet this section of the play is also full of suspense because each character also appears to be free to give or withhold his assent, and may, we feel – perhaps, just for this performance – choose not to co-operate. Shakespeare's emphasis on temperament as the cause of the tragedy appears in the stress he places on acts of choice by the major characters. Practically every scene involves the making of choices. The second scene is devoted almost entirely to Cassius's attempts to persuade Brutus to join the conspiracy and, as it moves towards its close, Brutus seems on the very verge of choice. The balanced clauses of his sentences convey the precarious equilibrium within his mind:

> That you do love me, I am nothing jealous;
> What you would work me to, I have some aim;
> How I have thought of this, and of these times,
> I shall recount hereafter. . . .
>   . . . What you have said
> I will consider; what you have to say
> I will with patience hear.   (I ii 162–5; 167–9)

His final statement of his position, cautiously defined, suggests that he is about to accede to Cassius's persuasions:

> Till then, my noble friend, chew upon this:
> Brutus had rather be a villager

> Than to repute himself a son of Rome
> Under these hard conditions as this time
> Is like to lay upon us.   (ɪ ii 171–5)

We feel it will only be a matter of time before he decides to join the alliance and, indeed, when he next appears, he reveals that he has made the choice Cassius predicted of him:

> It must be by his death.   (ɪɪ i 10)

The encounter between Caesar, Calphurnia and the conspirators which takes place immediately before the assassination is also a scene of persuasion and choice. Caesar's decision whether or not to go to the Capitol is shown to rest entirely on the interpretation he chooses to place on his wife's dream. Calphurnia herself interprets her vision of the statue issuing blood as a premonition of catastrophe; Decius Brutus, on the other hand, flatteringly argues that it is a prefiguration of Caesar's benefits to Rome. Offered these alternative opinions, Caesar chooses to believe the false one and, on the strength of it, proceeds voluntarily towards what we know will be his death. Even when, within seconds of the assassination, he is handed a paper exposing all the details of the plot, he brushes it aside, not, as Plutarch tells us, because the streets were crowded, which would have been a case of simple mischance, but because he chooses to appear altruistic and public-spirited:

> What touches us ourself shall be last serv'd.

Everyone makes his choice not on the basis of the available evidence but because of the kind of person he is and the kind of person by whom he is influenced, and every choice turns out, in the event, to be disastrous. Had these people been different, Shakespeare implies, history itself would have been different, but so consistent are their characters that none of them could have acted otherwise. They are the kind of people who make such choices, an idea which Caesar has in mind when he remarks that lean and hungry men like Cassius are likely to be dangerous, and which Coriolanus exemplifies in his unflinching refusal to be 'false to his nature'. Shakespeare repeatedly considers the paradox whereby a man exercises an apparent freedom of will and yet is destined, by the inescapable nature of his personality, for a predetermined fate. The most profound analysis of this paradox is to be found in *Macbeth* where the hero is continually making free and independent choices – to murder Duncan, Banquo, Macduff's family – and yet, as the witches foretell, is destined to be destroyed. The tragic process whereby a man freely chooses his own destined ruin is at work in the histories as well as the tragedies.

Politicians like Cassius owe their success in controlling events, at least temporarily, to their shrewd estimate of people's character and their consequent skill in predicting how they will behave. Brutus has no aptitude for this kind of strategy – he misjudges Antony's intentions completely, with fatal consequences for himself – but for Cassius it is an instinct:

> Well, Brutus, thou art noble; yet, I see,
> Thy honourable metal may be wrought
> From that it is dispos'd. Therefore it is meet
> That noble minds keep ever with their likes;
> For who so firm that cannot be seduc'd?
> Caesar doth bear me hard; but he loves Brutus.
> If I were Brutus now and he were Cassius,
> He should not humour me.   (ɪ ii 307–14)

Decius Brutus also has the ability to work on others and rightly predicts that Caesar will be lured by flattery. This kind of insight is attributed in retrospect to Richard II who predicts that Northumberland's alliance with Bolingbroke will never last:

> There is a history in all men's lives,
> Figuring the nature of the times deceas'd;
> The which observ'd, a man may prophesy,
> With a near aim, of the main chance of things
> As yet not come to life, who in their seeds
> And weak beginning lie intreasured.
> Such things become the hatch and brood of time;
> And, by the necessary form of this,
> King Richard might create a perfect guess
> That great Northumberland, then false to him,
> Would of that seed grow to a greater falseness.
> *(2 Henry IV,* ɪɪɪ i 80–90)

The tragic 'necessity', or destiny, which creates the Percys' rebellion, like that which creates the assassination of Caesar, is produced, over the course of time, by the unique conjunction of the relevant personalities. 'Men at some time are masters of their fates', Cassius believes,

> The fault, dear Brutus, is not in our stars,
> But in ourselves, that we are underlings.

He is proved to be right but not in the sense he intended, since his own fall is a product of his character.

It may be objected that Shakespeare's characters are not actually the victims of this kind of psychological determinism and that they enjoy a real freedom of choice which gives them genuine control over their lives and countries. In practice, however, we are in no position to discover what decisions they might have made since we know no more about them than Shakespeare allows us to see, and their decisions are so consistent with their characters that men like Cassius can predict exactly how they will behave. Nor is the action of *Julius Caesar* unaffected by simple mischance. It is this which gives to Cinna the poet the name of a conspirator and which brings him into the market place at the very time when the mob are thirsty for blood. These tragic ironies are given further weight by the blurring of fact and fiction. Knowing that the characters on the stage represent historical figures, we are partially persuaded that we are watching actual events as they occur and not fictions created for our entertainment. Shakespeare's view of history seems to be confirmed by history itself and to be a comment on the world in which we are still living. It is that much more persuasive.

The presence in the history plays of this kind of fortune, this destiny which ensures that the combination of certain kinds of character must produce certain consequences, is a feature which links them with the tragedies. The effect on one another of Othello, Iago and Desdemona must, we feel, have no other result than the death of Desdemona, an intimation which we sense most powerfully when Iago's temptation of Othello begins to develop its own momentum and becomes, as it were, independent and separated from any initial motivation Iago may have had. This sense of the force of destiny may well induce us to search into its nature and motives, to enquire what may be that 'ultimate power' which, as Bradley pointed out, perplexes the characters in *King Lear*. Although, incidentally, *Othello* is a less 'metaphysical' tragedy than *Lear*, nevertheless Othello himself comes almost to the point of asking this kind of question when, just before his death, he asks his witnesses,

> Will you, I pray, demand that demi-devil
> Why he hath thus ensnar'd my soul and body?   (v ii 304–5)

In other words he finds Iago's villainy incomprehensible in terms of what he – and, no doubt, we – regards as purely human, psychological motivation; a few moments earlier he has suspected that Iago may literally be the devil. He receives no answer to his question, nor, as we have remarked, are we given any consistent answers to the metaphysical questions posed in *King Lear*. In the history plays, however, such questions are very seldom asked, at any rate by the characters, who continue to behave as though they were free agents, wholly in charge of their destinies. An audience is, however, conscious that the events it is witnessing could develop in no other way, yet is supplied with no reliable information about their ultimate, teleological origin. The 'ultimate power' which directs Richard and Bolingbroke, or Brutus, Cassius and Caesar into the same orbit is unknowable. All we can say of it is that, if it exists, it acts in opposition to the wills of these characters (for even Bolingbroke's success turns out to be a kind of failure), that it produces results other than those they intend and that it limits their freedom of action. It is of this power that Mark Antony sees himself a victim, destined to failure by the very quality of his own temperament:

> But when we in our viciousness grow hard –
> O misery on't! – the wise gods seel our eyes,
> In our own filth drop our clear judgements, make us
> Adore our errors, laugh at's while we strut
> To our confusion.   (*Antony and Cleopatra*, iii xiii 111–15)

One can understand why, in the circumstances, Antony should arrive at such a despairing conviction, but we have no means of knowing whether, in Shakespeare's own mind, he is right. I shall return to this question in the next chapter.

The impression that Shakespeare's characters have a restricted freedom of choice and act in ignorance of their fates is given additional force by the order in which the dramatist arranges events. We have already seen him, in the episode leading to Salisbury's death, deploying his material in order to create ironies at the expense of his characters and he does so repeatedly in the later histories. During the early scenes of *Julius Caesar* we see little of Caesar himself but are given full access to the details of the conspiracy. By the time the conspirators meet Caesar to take him to the Capitol, he is practically the only person in the theatre who knows nothing of it and is led off like a lamb to the slaughter. The innocent, genial good nature with which he treats his 'friends' appears disastrously misplaced and we can only pity a victim who co-operates so willingly in his own assassination. Similarly we are shown Prince Hal formally acknowledging the authority of the Lord Chief Justice before we see Falstaff hurrying off to London, vowing destruction to the very man who will imprison him. Shakespeare's careful organisation of his material also shows us Coriolanus forming an alliance with Aufidius before we see the Tribunes in Rome congratulating themselves that they are safely rid of him. The playwright's dramatic strategy is simple enough to perceive and its effect is to reduce the stature of his characters by emphasising the disastrous limitations of their knowledge and the futility of their attempts to control events which are too complex for them to deal with. So ignorant are Caesar and Falstaff and the Tribunes of the real nature of their opponents that they unknowingly assist in their own calamities. The audience find themselves in the position of trapped spectators, foreseeing the course of destiny but unable to prevent it, and they experience a painful combination of anxiety and powerlessness comparable in kind, if not in degree, to the effect produced by *Othello*.

There is, moreover, a kind of irony which is unique to the history plays. In creating it Shakespeare again exploits the knowledge which his audience possesses, but it is a knowledge which he has no need to provide for them because they bring it with them into the theatre. The major events which Shakespeare dramatised, such as the deposition of Richard II, the assassination of Julius Caesar and the enthrallment of Antony by Cleopatra are historical facts familiar to everyone, including Shakespeare's first audiences who knew about them not just from history books but from poems and plays written before Shakespeare's. He uses this kind of hindsight to create the strong but simple irony which overshadows Cressida's vow of fidelity to Troilus and the subtler intimations of disaster which accompany the ostensibly harmonious conclusion of *Henry V*. During the peace conference with which that play ends, the French queen expresses the hope that their meeting will 'change all griefs and quarrels into love', and the French king, similarly, prays that the 'dear conjunction' of Henry and his daughter will 'plant neighbourhood and Christian-like accord' in their two countries. It scarcely needs the epilogue to remind us how vain these hopes will prove to be. The very expression of them creates a tragic irony which Shakespeare could have omitted had he chosen to do so. Our foreknowledge of the feeble government of Henry's son casts a similar cloud over the King's cheerful assumption that his bride will prove 'a good soldier-breeder':

> KING Shall not thou and I, between Saint Denis and Saint George, compound a boy, half French, half English, that shall go to Constantinople and take the Turk by the beard? Shall we not? What say'st thou, my fair flower-de-luce?
> KATHERINE I do not know dat.
> KING No: 'tis hereafter to know.   (v ii 203–10)

At moments such as these, our confidence in Henry's achievement is qualified by a pity for his human limitations. The history plays are full of characters who look forward to rewards we know they will not win, who make promises we know they will not keep and pursue what we know to be their own destruction. We foresee that the murder of Caesar, far from initiating a period of 'Liberty, freedom and enfran- chisement', will imminently create a civil war, and that the marriage of Antony to Octavia, as Enobarbus predicts, will not form a 'band which ties the friendship' of the triumvirs, but will prove 'the very strangler of their amity'. Such tragic processes seem inevitable be- cause we know in advance that they will happen. The effect is close to the one described by Aristotle when he argues that 'whereas we are not yet sure as to the possibility of that which has not happened, that which has happened is manifestly possible, else it would not have come to pass'.[15] We are dealing here, however, with something more like probability or inevitability: Shakespeare's characters seem to oppose themselves not so much against their fellow-men as against a destiny to whose purposes only their creator and ourselves have access, and which is foreshadowed in the prophetic utterances of soothsayers, prophetesses, witches and the sound of the departure of the god Hercules. It is this force, the power of fate working through history, to which Octavius Caesar refers when he advises his sister

> Be you not troubled with the time, which drives
> O'er your content these strong necessities,
> But let determin'd things to destiny
> Hold unbewail'd their way.   (*Antony and Cleopatra*, iii vi 82–5)

He here apparently sees himself as the agent of destiny and, knowing the outcome of the tragedy, we are inclined to agree with him.

Some of Shakespeare's characters, feeling themselves threatened by the march of events, turn to the consolation of philosophy. If they are unable to attain a place in the world, they can at least reassure themselves that the mind is its own place. This is the consolation to which each of the rival kings, Henry VI and Edward IV, turns when he is temporarily thrown out of office. 'My crown is in my heart' says Henry when he is forced to retreat into hiding;

> Not deck'd with diamonds and Indian stones,
> Nor to be seen. My crown is call'd content;
> A crown it is that seldom kings enjoy.   (*3 Henry VI*, iii i 62–5)

Then when, by one of the sudden turns of fortune typical of these plays, Henry is thrust back into power, it is his rival, Edward's, turn to assert,

> Though fortune's malice overthrow my state,
> My mind exceeds the compass of her wheel.   (iv iii 46–7)

This kind of stoical resignation is, however, adopted only as a last resort and, as a retreat from the onslaughts of fortune, it is only temporary. A further turn of the wheel brings each of them back into the struggle. The only complete escape is through the stoical act of suicide which Cleopatra chooses when she realises how paltry it is to be 'Fortune's knave, a minister of her will'.

The effect of fortune, whether it reveals itself as destiny or simple luck, is to frustrate the ambitions of men, and if the history plays prove anything it is that human hopes are very seldom realised, or, as Samuel Johnson declared, 'the natural flights of the human mind are not from pleasure to pleasure but from hope to hope'.[16] *Henry VI Part I* concludes with Suffolk's triumphant success in winning Margaret as a bride for the King, and his determination to rule 'both her, the King and realm'. In the next part he is banished and murdered by an obscure sailor. The Duchess of Gloucester has aspirations to be queen, but is compelled to parade as a penitent through the public streets on her way into exile. Her husband, convinced that his innocence will protect him, dismisses her warnings that he himself will fall, but is promptly accused of treason and murdered in his bed. The rebel Jack Cade hopes to establish a new society in which there is common ownership of land, but is accidentally captured and killed by a smallholder. York's son encourages his father to think, like Tamburlaine,

> How sweet a thing it is to wear a crown,
> Within whose circuit is Elysium.   (*3 Henry VI*, I ii 29–30)

But the only crown York wears is a paper one, mockingly placed on his head by his enemies before they stab him. It is not Bolingbroke who fulfills his vow to make a pilgrimage to the Holy Land, but, as Robert Ornstein points out, his former rival Mowbray, whereas Bolingbroke dies merely in the Jerusalem chamber.[17] In the light of such narratives *de casibus virorum illustrium*, Agamemnon's assertion that men's hopes are inevitably thwarted by the opposition of fortune or great Jove reads like an axiom which history everywhere supports:

> The ample proposition that hope makes
> In all designs begun on earth below
> Fails in the promis'd largeness.
> (*Troilus and Cressida*, I iii 3–5)

Troilus and Cressida is obviously not the only history play to support this conviction.

Nor can such ironic reversals of fortune be attributed to some kind of divine providence or poetic justice which punishes men for their crimes. Edward, the child Prince of Wales, is brought to London ostensibly for his coronation but actually to be murdered. Neither he nor his precocious brother nor young Rutland nor the well-meaning old Humphrey of Gloucester can possibly be said to deserve their deaths. Conversely, though most of Queen Margaret's guilty associates die violently, the terrible queen herself survives to a ripe old age. It would take the skill of a casuist or a Shakespearean scholar to demonstrate a pattern of divine justice in punishments as random as these.

What is at work is the power of fortune as Boethius describes it:

> Harsh punishment, deserved by the criminal, afflicts the innocent.
> Immoral scoundrels now occupy positions of power and unjustly
> trample the rights of good men. Virtue, which ought to shine forth,
> is covered up and hides in darkness, while good men suffer for the
> crimes of the wicked . . . O God, whoever you are who joins all
> things in perfect harmony, look down upon this miserable earth!
> We men are no small part of Your great work, yet we wallow here in
> the stormy sea of fortune.[18]

Very few of Shakespeare's characters, however, are content, or even
allowed, to adopt Boethius's attitude to fortune and seek the paradise
within themselves. The history plays, as is well known, portray a long
line of political adventurers who put their hands to fortune's wheel
and attempt to turn it in their favour. They include Suffolk, York and
Warwick in the early histories, Richard III, Bolingbroke, Falstaff,
Prince Hal, Cassius, Mark Antony as he appears in *Julius Caesar*,
Octavius and Ulysses. All of them believe, with good reason, that the
way to gain control of fortune is to penetrate and influence the minds
of other people, and one way of looking at the history plays is to see
them as the record of attempts by individuals to shape history in
accordance with their own wills. The difficulty of the enterprise is apparent from the fact that very few of them – Henry V and Octavius
Caesar are perhaps the only ones – achieve any lasting success.

It is likely that Shakespeare was familiar with the teachings of
Machiavelli either at first hand or by report,[19] and *The Prince* reads repeatedly like a manual of instruction studied by Shakespeare's politicians. A. H. Gilbert has shown that many of Machiavelli's maxims
are similar to those delivered by the authors of medieval books of
advice to princes,[20] but what makes Machiavelli particularly relevant
to the history plays is his unique preoccupation with fortune which,
as Gilbert says, 'pervades *The Prince* as she does no other similar
work':

> She is ever present; few of the chapters are without references to
> Fortune or associated matters such as occasion, chance, time as
> 'the mother of many mutations', or the variable things of the world.
> This dotting of the pages with references to mutability shows the
> author's preoccupation in his advice to the ruler; the work is, as it

were, an exhortation to be ready against the uncertainty of the future. This is a world of flux and reflux; times of prosperity must be looked on not as normal, but as opportunities in which the wise man will prepare for the deluge.[21]

Richard of Gloucester, the most successful of Shakespeare's early adventurers, specifically associates himself with Machiavelli in his first great soliloquy where he asserts that he can 'set the murderous Machiavel to school' (*3 Henry VI*, iii ii 193), but he has revealed his natural impulse to challenge and resist fortune much earlier, when he responds to the news of his father's horrifying murder:

> But in this troublous time what's to be done?
> Shall we go throw away our coats of steel
> And wrap our bodies in black mourning-gowns,
> Numbering our Ave-Maries with our beads?
> Or shall we on the helmets of our foes
> Tell our devotion with revengeful arms?
> If for the last, say 'Ay', and to it, lords   (ii i 159–65)

Both nature and fortune have been unfavourable to Richard from the start, for he has been born deformed and is kept from the crown by prior claimants such as his elder brother and the King's own children. His remedy is characteristically crude: 'to hew my way out with a bloody axe'. The impulse to revenge, incidentally, which motivates the young Richard in common with several characters in the histories, takes it for granted that they can successfully resist the power of fortune.

The first stage in his rise to power, the murder of his brother Clarence, is successful because he manages to escape the blame for it and to appear so blandly good-humoured that even his poor victim is taken in. He continues to appear cheerfully ingenuous in the eyes of others right up to the murder of Hastings who, within minutes of his arrest, still believes

> there's never a man in Christendom
> Can lesser hide his love or hate than he;
> For by his face straight shall you know his heart.   (iii iv 53–5)

After each successive murder, however, he is less able to preserve his appearance of honest piety. Queen Margaret, who has experienced his butcher's methods in an earlier play, is never taken in by him and her curses are really cries for a vengeance she no longer has the power to carry out. As the number of Richard's crimes accumulates, she is joined by the other dowagers, all 'hungry for vengeance' on one another and the King, and the sense of outrage and fear spreads among the citizens of London. Thus Richard's barbarity, far from securing his position, actually propels his subjects into opposition and the basic pattern of the play is one of murder and revenge, not, as in the case of *Macbeth*, crime and punishment. To this extent, as R. G. Moulton pointed out, the action of *Richard III* resembles those of the three parts of *Henry VI* to which it forms a climax and conclusion. The three earlier histories show a repeated pattern of ascents to power by bloody methods, by men like Suffolk and York, which spontaneously provoke revenge, a system, as Moulton describes it, 'by which those who triumph in one nemesis become the victims of the next; so that the whole suggests a "chain of destruction" like that binding together the orders of the brute creation which live by preying upon one another'.[22] Margaret's lamentations thus open up 'a vista of nemeses receding further and further back into history'.[23] In the context of the three preceding plays, Richard's defeat appears as a final nemesis. His ascent to power entails the familiar penalty of outraging those who survive his victims, and he dies unrevenged because he has long since forfeited everyone's sympathy; he rightly foresees that, on his death, no soul will pity him. The ghosts who haunt his sleep on the night before battle are less like the voices of his troubled conscience than a chorus of revengers undermining him from within:

> Methought the souls of all that I had murder'd
> Came to my tent, and every one did threat
> To-morrow's vengeance on the head of Richard.   (v iii 205–7)

His complaint, 'there is no creature loves me' is self-pitying but it is also a comment on his failure as a politician. Richard is not even a good Machiavellian: he ignores Machiavelli's advice to the ruler to 'conciliate friends' and make himself 'loved by his subjects'.[24] Contrary to his beliefs, he can teach Machiavelli nothing.

Bolingbroke, on his own admission, is a great deal subtler. He acquires the throne not by terrorism but by a 'humble and familiar courtesy' designed, as he confesses, to 'pluck allegiance from men's hearts'. Some of this 'candy deal of courtesy' is actually shown in his treatment of Hotspur shortly after his return to England:

> I count myself in nothing else so happy
> As in a soul rememb'ring my good friends;
> And as my fortune ripens with thy love,
> It shall be still thy true love's recompense.

(Richard II, II iii 46–9)

Once brought to power, however, he ceases to ingratiate himself with Northumberland and Hotspur, and his former solicitude to please them appears false, as it probably was. He is one of those rulers described by Machiavelli who cannot keep the friendship of those who have helped them to power.[25] The feigned humility of this 'king of smiles' has one thing in common with the brutality of Richard III: the method each uses to secure his position eventually weakens it, a characteristically Shakespearean irony.

Only Henry V succeeds in winning the love of his people and he does so by methods even more devious than his father's. As the King's son, of course, he has fortune on his side, but he avoids being thought a criminal by committing no really serious crimes, and escapes his father's reputation for sycophancy by not apparently caring what people think of him. His performance is so successful that even his own father is taken in: it is ironical that Henry IV gives political advice to the one man who least needs it. Paradoxically Prince Hal's feigned profligacy is, in the long run, politically effective whereas Henry VI's genuine piety is obviously not. He is, moreover, not simply the most successful of Shakespeare's political adventurers, but the one who most closely follows the advice of Machiavelli, for he knows better than earlier Shakespearean rulers how essential it is 'for a prince who would maintain his position, to have learned how to be other than good, and to use or not to use his goodness as necessity requires'.[26]

Hal owes his success largely to his understanding of the people and his ability to manipulate their feelings towards him, which is what his spurious reformation is all about ('spurious' in the sense that he is not a genuine sinner). It also depends on his scrupulous understanding of himself and his strict fulfilment of the career he has planned. However spontaneous his enjoyment of Falstaff's company may be – and it seems genuine enough – he is always able to terminate it when the need arises. Falstaff, another aspiring Machiavellian, believes that he can understand and control the prince, but is actually unable to control himself. His intermittent and maudlin resolutions to reform never come to anything, whereas Hal keeps his vows to the letter. Hence, while Hal can imitate the sun, Falstaff continues to be governed by the moon, the agent of fortune.

Henry V is one of the very few characters in the history plays who manages to control his fortune; Octavius Caesar is probably the only other and we see far less of him at work. The Chorus, who overlooks many of the subtleties in *Henry V*, is wrong to claim that 'Fortune made his sword': he forged it for himself. He is, however, the exception to the rule, and even this 'star of England' very soon falls victim either to 'the bad revolting stars' or 'the subtle-witted French', depending on whether you believe that fortune or men were the cause of his death. His political achievement collapses with him.

What Shakespeare sees, as he looks back over the history of Troy, Rome and medieval England, is largely the spectacle of human failure. Successful leaders like Henry VII and Octavius Caesar are dull, remote figures in comparison with Richard II, Bolingbroke and Antony whose agonised sense of failure interested him much more. The striking fact about Henry V's achievement is that exceptional intelligence and subtlety were needed to accomplish it and, for this reason, it is in Shakespeare's eyes unique. It is probably a mistake to search the plays for any consistent, systematic theory of fortune. But if we look beyond the outmoded terminology and the medieval trappings of the wheel, the ball and the blindfold goddess, we can perceive in them an attempt to externalise and define the conviction that men's hopes are constantly thwarted and that they blindly pursue the means of their own defeat. The persistence with which images of fortune recur throughout medieval European literature, in allegorical poems, chronicles and handbooks as well as in visual art, shows that this potentially tragic view of man was held over a long period. It was an idea which Shakespeare received from his immediate past. The idea which we find in Boccaccio, Lydgate and Milton that fortune arrived in the world as a result of the fall of Adam is a way of explaining why failure and disappointment are necessary features of the human condition. The fulfilment of human hopes was possible only in the world before the Fall. Shakespeare's historical characters struggle with their limited capacities to regain it but the plays imply that it has been irrecoverably lost.

4 | *Prayer, Prophecy and Providence*

History as Shakespeare portrays it is determined either by the simple kind of fortune, or 'chance', which intervenes chiefly in war or by the more complex fate, or 'destiny', which operates through a combination of characters, as in the psychological conflicts which precede the deposition of Richard II or the assassination of Julius Caesar. Many of Shakespeare's politicians attempt to control the otherwise arbitrary effects of fortune by the exercise of a Machiavellian ingenuity which gives them mastery over their fellow-men, but even if, like Henry IV or Henry V, they are successful for a time, they are still helpless in the face of old age and death which reduces them and their achievements to nothing. The minor characters in the history plays, such as Iden, the Lord Mayor and citizens of London, Cinna the poet and Cleopatra's waiting-women, vividly create a sense of the nation whose history is being depicted, but their fates depend upon those of the people who govern them.

In their attempts to shape the world in accordance with their own desires, Shakespeare's characters have an ultimate resource on which some of them draw in situations of extreme peril or defeat and that is supernatural aid, the assistance of God. The portrayal of prayer in extreme crisis and the dramatic ironies which accompany such appeals is another feature of the history plays which connects them with the tragedies, and it may be illuminating first to look at two such episodes in the tragedies before we consider the implications of prayer in the histories.

The hero of Shakespeare's first tragedy, *Titus Andronicus*, is subjected to a process of extreme and prolonged suffering in which he is powerless either to retaliate or find redress. Having endured the loss of nearly all his children, and the horrors of his daughter's rape and the severing of her arms, he is told that two of his remaining sons have been condemned to death. He agrees to a bloody bargain with his enemies, cutting off his own hand on the understanding that this self-inflicted mutilation will save his sons' lives. He then calls on the gods to take pity on him:

> O' here I lift this one hand up to heaven,
> And bow this feeble ruin to the earth;
> If any power pities wretched tears,
> To that I call!   (III i 207–10)

His outraged sense of justice and his frustration that his torturers are unpunished compel him to protest to heaven and, in his half-feigned insanity, he shoots arrows up into the sky petitioning the gods for relief. The message they carry is *Terras Astræa reliquit*, 'Justice has left the earth', the words used by Ovid in his account of the ending of the Golden Age.[1]

Finding no justice in the world, he decides,

> We will solicit heaven, and move the gods
> To send down Justice for to wreak our wrongs.   (IV iii 50–1)

The despair which motivates this bizarre gesture is comparable to that experienced by Albany in *King Lear* when he foresees a time of general carnage which only divine intervention can prevent:

> If that the heavens do not their visible spirits
> Send quickly down to tame these vile offences,
> It will come
> Humanity must perforce prey on itself,
> Like monsters of the deep.   (IV ii 46–50)

The gestures which Titus and Albany make are wrung from them in situations of extreme barbarity which seem to have gone beyond human control. Their prayers are appeals to the gods, made when human efforts seem futile, but they have no apparent effect: the trage-dies run their courses and the justice for which they appeal is a very rough one, destroying the innocent and guilty alike.

Most of Shakespeare's history plays were written between *Titus Andronicus* and *King Lear* and they also contain situations of extreme injustice, the victims of which, despairing of human remedies, call on heaven for help. The three *Henry VI* plays are full of scenes of great cruelty comparable to those in the tragedies, such as the death of Talbot as he holds his dead son in his arms, the daubing of the captive York in his son's blood and the appearance before Henry VI of the son who has unwittingly killed his father and the father who has killed his son. The father carrying, like Talbot and Lear, his dead child, exclaims to heaven for compassion:

> O' pity, God, this miserable age!
> What stratagems, how fell, how butcherly,
> Erroneous, mutinous and unnatural
> This deadly quarrel daily doth beget! (*3 Henry VI*, ii v 88–91)

His prayer has no apparent effect, for the civil war continues and the King, who has observed the scene, is immediately caught up again in the conflict. If prayer is a desperate attempt to restore peace and justice to the world it is an attempt which, at any rate in these contexts, fails, for the world of the history plays like those of *Lear* and *Titus* is one from which the gods appear to be absent. The mother of the princes murdered by Richard III accuses God of sleeping when the deed was done, and Richard II soon discovers that God sends no angels to protect him against his enemies.

Such invocations, moving and pitiful in themselves, are accompanied by a terrible irony derived from the contexts in which they are delivered. After Titus has bartered his hand for his sons' lives and called on the pity of the gods, a messenger enters carrying his sons' heads; after Goneril and Regan have been destroyed through what Albany believes to be 'the judgement of the heavens', Lear enters with Cordelia's body; after the father's plea to God to take pity on the 'miserable age', the civil war continues; after Richard II's confident expression of trust in divine protection, news arrives of the defection of his subjects to Bolingbroke. Such ironies seem to have been created by Shakespeare in order to show that history is a purely secular affair in which men can expect no supernatural aid. Ironies of a less shocking kind, though with similar implications, are also created by the contexts in which his historical characters give thanks to heaven for their blessings, as in Henry VI's thanksgiving for his bride, Margaret, on her arrival in England. At this point in the play, Henry is ignorant both of the circumstances which preceded the arrival of Margaret and of the calamities which will ensue as a consequence of their marriage.

Unlike Henry, the audience knows that the marriage has been contrived by the ambitious Suffolk in the hope that, through his power over the Queen, he will be able to rule the country. The audience also observes, immediately after the arrival of Margaret, the apprehensions of the nobility, justified in the event, that the marriage will prove disastrous for England. Henry's prayer, however touching in itself, is therefore overshadowed by disturbing ironies which cast doubt on his faith and the existence of the kind of providential deity in whom he trusts:

> O Lord, that lends me life,
> Lend me a heart replete with thankfulness!
> For thou hast given me in this beauteous face
> A world of earthly blessings to my soul,
> If sympathy of love unite our thoughts.   (*2 Henry VI*, i i 19–23)

Deceived about his bride's true nature, Henry also appears deceived about the god whom he believes to have sent her. In spite of the suffering he endures during his reign, he maintains his faith in a personal god, the existence of which is steadily challenged by events, with the result that his trust increasingly appears misplaced: his innocence is subjected to continual ironies. Towards the end of his reign, after he has been temporarily thrown out of office by the Yorkists, he thanks God and God's agent, Warwick, for restoring him to the throne:

> But, Warwick, after God, thou set'st me free,
> And chiefly, therefore, I thank God and thee;
> He was the author, thou the instrument.
> (*3 Henry VI*, iv vi 16–18)

His belief that his restoration is the work of providence would have few ironical implications were it not for the dramatic context in which Shakespeare has placed his words, for a few moments earlier, in the preceding scene, we have seen Henry's rival, Edward, escape from captivity and hurry away to seize the crown, an attempt which shortly proves successful. In these circumstances Henry has little to be thankful for and the ironies which surround his words again make his faith appear foolish.

Politicians whose religious attitude is very much more sceptical than Henry's find it to their advantage to give thanks in public to a deity who has, as they well know, played no part in their devious or criminal activities. Richard of Gloucester hypocritically thanks the Lord for his humility between his completion of one murder and his arrangement of the next; Cardinal Beaufort, having conspired to destroy his life-long enemy, receives the announcement of his murder with the bland comment, 'God's secret judgement'. It is of this kind of religious hypocrisy that Prince John accuses the well-intentioned rebel Archbishop Scroop, but Scroop is no such cynic: the real hypocrite is Prince John himself. With a half-lie he induces Scroop to dismiss his soldiers and promptly condemns him to the block. The Prince's comment on this devious victory is wholly disingenuous:

> God, and not we, hath safely fought today. (*2 Henry IV*, iv ii 121)

This is simply an attempt to cover up his duplicity by attributing his success to the almighty. In fact the more we examine as a whole the invocations to God with which the history plays abound, the more apparent it becomes that he is fashioned by Shakespeare's characters in their own image and saddled with any responsibilities they are unable, or unwilling to undertake for themselves: Henry VI's tendency to leave the government of England in the hands of God is a sign of his own incompetence.* Queen Margaret takes little interest in the almighty so long as she is in office, but when she is old and powerless she continually appeals to heaven as an instrument of revenge, or what Wilbur Sanders nicely calls 'a supernatural agency under contractual obligation to exterminate the house of York'.[2] When it seems that God has actually fulfilled her curses, she attributes to him a barbarism that is exclusively her own:

> O upright, just, and true-disposing God,
> How do I thank thee that this carnal cur
> Preys on the issue of his mother's body
> And makes her pew-fellow with others' moan!
>
> (*Richard III*, iv iv 55–8)

In a series of plays where God's name is played with so irresponsibly, it is difficult to be wholly convinced by Richmond's claim to be the instrument of divine justice. It is impossible to share

---

* See, for example, his reaction to the news that the French territories are totally lost: 'Cold news, Lord Somerset; but God's will be done' (*2 Henry VI*, iii i 86)

Tillyard's confident belief that Richmond is 'utterly God's minister, as he claims to be' if only because we have heard similar claims before and concluded that this is a world in which men have to fend for themselves. Richmond is certainly not portrayed as a hypocrite and his prayer before battle is offered in all honesty, but it would be easier to believe in his crusading mission if we knew more about him and about his motives for mounting the invasion. But these are never revealed, perhaps because Shakespeare thought it advisable not to enquire into them (Richmond was, after all, the grandfather of the reigning monarch) and he is not so much a positive moral force as the leader of an opposition which Richard has created. The spirits of Richard's victims may assure him, in words uncomfortably like Richard II's, that 'God and good angels' will fight on his side, but Richmond is pragmatic enough to know that only if his soldiers themselves crush down the helmets of their adversaries will they live to praise God for their victory (v iii 108–14). Richmond is only one of many characters who call on God to carry out their wishes: he differs from the others to the extent that his cause is successful. But in these plays not all well-deserving prayers are answered and we have no means of knowing whether his victory is achieved with divine assistance or not. All we can say is that Richmond has a genuine faith in providence which he shares with other characters, like Henry VI, whose trust is treated ironically. Hall, whose chronicle was the main source for *Richard III* is, incidentally, just as non-committal on this subject as Shakespeare: the most he ventures to say about Richmond's victory and marriage is that peace '*was thought* to discende oute of heaven into England'.[3]

Henry V makes petitions and gives thanks to God more frequently than any Shakespearean character, but the attitude we are supposed to adopt towards his religious protestations is extremely difficult to assess. This is partly because Holinshed, Shakespeare's principal source, believed that Henry was a genuinely saintly monarch and the piety of Holinshed's portrait has found its way into the play (in the attitude of the Chorus, for example); partly because, throughout the three plays in which he appears, Henry is such an accomplished performer that it is hard to know when he is being sincere; and partly because in *Henry V* he is almost entirely a public figure playing to an audience of diplomats or soldiers. And, of course, unlike most of Shakespeare's characters, he finds that his petitions have apparently been granted.

It is impossible not to recall that Henry's invasion of France is undertaken in order to secure national unity by distracting the minds of potential rebels at home. The expedition is made in accordance with his father's advice, that he should

> busy giddy minds
> With foreign quarrels, that action, hence borne out,
> May waste the memory of the former days.
>
> (*2 Henry IV*, iv v 214–16)

This kind of foreign invasion, deliberately embarked upon in order to secure domestic peace, is one of the stratagems recommended by Machiavelli, who warns his royal pupil that 'when affairs are quiet abroad, a Prince has to fear that they [i.e. his subjects] may engage in secret plots'.[4] He commends Ferdinand of Aragon for his astuteness in avoiding subversion by this method:

> In the beginning of his reign he made war on Granada, which enter-prise was the foundation of his power. At first he carried on the war leisurely, without fear of interruption, and kept the minds of the Barons of Castile so completely occupied with it that they had no time to think of changes at home . . . With the money of the church and of his subjects he was able to maintain his armies, and during the prolonged contest to lay the foundations of that military excel-lence which afterwards made him famous. Moreover, to enable him to engage in still greater undertakings, always covering himself with the cloak of religion, he had recourse to what may be called *pious cruelty*, in driving out and clearing his Kingdom of the Moors.[5]

By following the advice of Machiavelli and his own father, Henry V is obviously successful in distracting the minds of potential rebels and securing national unity. Whether his enterprise is defensible morally is another matter. As the son of a usurper his right to rule England is dubious, as he well knows, and this in turn casts doubts on his claim to France. It is true that, before he sets out on the expedition, Henry scrupulously interrogates the Archbishop on this question:

> And God forbid, my dear and faithful lord,
> That you should fashion, wrest, or bow your reading,
> Or nicely charge your understanding soul
> With opening titles miscreate, whose right

> Suits not in native colours with the truth;
> For God doth know how many, now in health,
> Shall drop their blood in approbation
> Of what your reverence shall incite us to.
> Therefore take heed how you impawn our person,
> How you awake our sleeping sword of war.   (ɪ ii 13–22)

His assumption that many 'shall' drop their blood and that his sleeping sword actually will 'awake' strongly suggests, however, that he is already determined on invasion. The Archbishop's long and devious exposition of the Salic Law thus appears a needless, even ridiculous, justification of what had already been decided.

It is in this morally disturbing context that Henry makes the following protestation to the French ambassadors:

> But this lies all within the will of God,
> To whom I do appeal; and in whose name,
> Tell you the Dauphin, I am coming on,
> To venge me as I may and to put forth
> My rightful hand in a well-hallow'd cause.   (ɪ ii 289–93)

He is here either, like the characters in the early histories, sincerely creating a god in his own image, or hypocritically invoking him to justify a morally dubious cause. The audience, having observed Henry's dealings with the churchmen, is conscious of ironies hidden from the Dauphin's emissaries, but of which he himself is, perhaps, aware.

There are disturbing ironies, too, in Henry's public announcement that God has revealed the treachery of the three disloyal peers. The first an audience hears of Cambridge, Scroop and Grey, before they appear on the stage, is that their plot to assassinate the King has already been uncovered by Henry's intelligence agents (ɪɪ ii 6–7), and knowing that he is already informed of their treacherous design, we are able to admire the skill with which he stage-manages their public confession of guilt: the unfortunate traitors are so stunned by the revelation that they think it has been brought about by a miracle, and they go off to their execution cheerfully:

> Our purposes God justly hath discover'd,
> And I repent my fault more than my death.   (ɪɪ ii 151–2)

Never did faithful subject more rejoice
At the discovery of most dangerous treason
Than I do at this hour joy o'er myself,
Prevented from a damned enterprise.   (II ii 161–4)

The audience, however, already warned of Henry's intentions, knows that the miracle has been contrived. Henry's control of the situation is masterly, but he lets the traitors go to their deaths under the impression that God alone has brought their crimes to light, and he is, moreover, quick to interpret the 'miracle' as a sign that the Lord is on his side in the forthcoming expedition:

Now, lords, for France; the enterprise whereof
Shall be to you as us like glorious.
We doubt not of a fair and lucky war,
Since God so graciously hath brought to light
This dangerous treason, lurking in our way
To hinder our beginnings; we doubt not now
But every rub is smoothed on our way.
Then forth, dear countrymen; let us deliver
Our puissance into the hand of God,
Putting it straight in expedition.   (II ii 182–91)

In its context, Henry's words are accompanied by ironies of which the King's subjects, but not a theatre audience, are unaware, and the ironies cast doubt on his sincerity and his avowed belief in a providential deity.

At first sight the dramatic impressions made by Henry's invocations of God's name before and after the Battle of Agincourt seem much more straightforward. This is the only time in the play when he is alone, expressing his inward thoughts and not thinking of the effect his words will have on other people. He is about to embark on what, in the play's terms, is the most critical enterprise of his career, the test for which his activities in the two previous plays have been a preparation. At this point he appeals to God to help him to overcome difficulties of which he is deeply aware: the fear with which his troops regard the enemy and his own sense of inherited guilt for his father's seizure of the throne. The motives behind his prayer are simple and genuine. In view of his apprehensions and the fact that his troops are greatly outnumbered by the enemy, it is logical that, after the battle, he should ascribe to God the strength which brought him victory:

> O God, thy arm was here!
> And not to us, but to thy arm alone
> Ascribe we all. When, without stratagem,
> But in plain shock and even play of battle,
> Was ever known so great and little loss
> On one part and on th'other? Take it, God,
> For it is none but thine.   (IV viii 104–10)

Yet we have just learned of the ten thousand French who have been slaughtered, and heard the names of their noblemen who lie dead in the field, and we may wonder at the nature of a God who promotes Henry's cause so devastatingly. This doubt, not about the sincerity but the validity of the King's religious belief, grows when we are told of the effects of the war on the French land and people by the Duke of Burgundy, a new character at this stage in the play, and one to whom we pay refreshed attention. His speech describes with moving particularity the devastation for which Henry and his soldiers are responsible:

> And as our vineyards, fallows, meads, and hedges,
> Defective in their natures, grow to wildness;
> Even so our houses and ourselves and children
> Have lost, or do not learn for want of time,
> The sciences that should become our country;
> But grow, like savages – as soldiers will,
> That nothing do but meditate on blood –
> To swearing and stern looks, diffus'd attire,
> And everything that seems unnatural.   (V ii 54–62)

In the light of this pitiful revelation it is difficult, in retrospect, to sympathise completely with the King in his attribution of the victory to God, for we realise, in intimately human terms, the price at which it has been gained.

An audience can react to Henry V's religious protestations in one of three ways: we may regard him, as Holinshed did, as a saintly ruler, genuinely assisted by divine providence; we may see him as a Cromwellian figure who acts in the belief that he is the instrument of God; or we may consider him a religious hypocrite who successfully turns any apparent sign of supernatural assistance to his own advantage. Although each of these interpretations has had its literary critical supporters, I believe that the first is untenable if only because so many of Henry's religious claims are made in contexts which overshadow them with ironies, and it is Shakespeare who creates the ironies; Holinshed is a great deal simpler.

Indeed it transpires that very few of the appeals or thanks to God which are spoken by Shakespeare's characters are free from ironies created by the dramatist. Saintly men like Henry VI offer thanks to God for blessings which we know will prove curses, evil women like Margaret praise God when their appetite for vengeance has been gratified, and the successful leader, Henry V, ascribes to God the victory in a campaign undertaken for morally dubious motives which we later learn has reduced his opponents' land to savagery. These characters are not all hypocrites and their prayers are often sincerely uttered. The prayers of some of them, such as the father who has killed his son, though offered in great extremity, have no apparent effect; the prayers of others, like Richmond and Henry V, are followed by success. Whether or not their victories are achieved by the power of God working through them, we are in no position to decide since we can not know what would have happened had they not appealed for divine assistance. Had Shakespeare been a novelist he would have had the opportunity to tell us, in his own person, whether Richmond and Henry were agents of divine providence or merely thought themselves to be so. As a dramatist, he simply portrays the tendency of people to seek God's help in times of stress and to attribute to God their successes, especially when they occur against all reasonable predictions. The need which Shakespeare's historical characters feel to pray to a dimly conceived supernatural power tends to emphasise their helplessness in the face of cruelty and injustice; the apparently random way in which their prayers are followed by failure or success tends to emphasise their ignorance of the ways of the deity who, they believe, controls their world. The role of God in the history plays is comparable to that of the gods in *King Lear*: men hold conflicting views of Him and He remains inscrutable. This gulf between men and God is forcefully expressed by the Duke of York during Bolingbroke's rebellion:

Comfort's in heaven; and we are on the earth.   (*Richard II*, ii ii 78)

It may be apparent by now that all the major topics I have discussed so far in these chapters are closely connected. To be exposed to the influence of fortune is one of the consequences of living in time, since it is in the nature of our temporality that we are ignorant of what the future has in store for us. To be caught up in time, to be subjected to the influence of fortune and to have continual anxieties about the future are all, according to treatments of the Genesis story, such as Milton's, consequences of the same initial sin. This complex of ideas is neatly expressed in a characteristically wry observation by Hall the chronicler who obviously shared Shakespeare's assumptions about the fallen nature of man:

> If men wer angels and foresaw thynges to com, they like beastes would not ronne to their confusion: but fortune which gideth the destiny of man, will turne her whele as she listeth, whosoever saith nay.[6]

This comment sums up many of the implications of the history plays, particularly in its emphasis on men's ignorance of the future. In this context, petitionary prayers may be seen as an ultimate attempt to shape the future in accordance with one's own wishes, as in Henry V's prayer before Agincourt. The energies of Shakespeare's Machiavellian adventurers, whether they are malevolent like Richard III or merely irresponsible like Falstaff, are directed towards a mastery of the future and, indeed, Machiavelli's own writings have been described by A. H. Gilbert as 'an exhortation to be ready against the uncertainty of the future'. (See page 49 above.) Only an audience, already acquainted with the actual course of events, knows to what gain or loss such energies are being expended. It is because of their preoccupation with the future that a significant part is played in the lives of Shakespeare's historical characters by seers, soothsayers, necromancers and prophets new inspired. Prophecy, like prayer, is grasped as a means of controlling history, and its value is, again, negligible.

Some of these forewarnings are not the expression of supernatural insight, but simply intelligent guesses based on the available evidence and are not different in kind from Cassius's prediction that Brutus will be persuaded to join the conspiracy. Richard II seems to be supernaturally inspired when he foretells the defection of Northumberland from Bolingbroke and the ensuing civil war:

> Northumberland, thou ladder wherewithal
> The mounting Bolingbroke ascends my throne,
> The time shall not be many hours of age
> More than it is, ere foul sin gathering head
> Shall break into corruption.   (*Richard II,* v i 55–9)

This warning turns out, of course, to be true, as Henry IV realises when he recalls Richard's words towards the end of the rebellion. According to Henry's counsellor, Warwick, however, Richard's warning was not genuinely prophetic but simply an intelligent guess, based on his insight into Northumberland's character. It is, incidentally, worth noting that Richard's warning did nothing to encourage any of his listeners to try and change the course of events; indeed it merely strengthens our impression, already discussed, that men are destined to certain courses of action by the inescapable nature of their characters. (See above, page 40.)

Other seers who make their appearance in the history plays do, however, have genuine gifts of prophecy since their predictions are made on no tangible evidence of what is going to happen. The soothsayers in *Julius Caesar* and *Antony and Cleopatra* have no precise knowledge of the future, but they do have vague intimations of disaster. Other inspired prophecies are the utterances of the spirit raised for the Duchess of Gloucester by the witch Margery Jourdain (*2 Henry VI,* I iv), the oracular cries of Cassandra foretelling the destruction of Troy (*Troilus and Cressida,* II ii 101–12) and Calphurnia's account of her dream during the night before her husband's assassination (*Julius Caesar,* II ii 75–82). This last example is also the simplest, in that Calphurnia's apprehensions are confirmed very quickly, and a brief analysis of its effect reveals the implications of prophecies of this kind. Calphurnia's dream, needless to say, conveys a strong impression that some supernatural power has an interest in events, especially since it is accompanied by other omens, thunder and lightning, comets and the rising of bodies from their graves. The impending murder, for which the audience is waiting, seems to be predestined by some powerful force in the universe with which Calphurnia has been in contact. Yet when Caesar sets out for the Capitol, he does not appear, at that particular point in the play, to be simply propelled there by an irresistible force. On the contrary, he is clearly lured there by the persuasions of the conspirators, and is even given an opportunity to decide for himself between the interpretation of the dream given by his wife and the contrary version given by Decius Brutus. The assassination, therefore, while it fulfils Calphurnia's prophecy, also seems to result from a free and independent act of choice by the victim. Examination of the more extended processes by which the prophecies of Cassandra and those of Margery Jourdain's spirits are fulfilled will, I believe, yield similar conclusions. The effect of this combination of prediction and choice is to make the characters appear voluntarily to co-operate in the working out of a fate which is in opposition to their own purposes. Even when a character deliberately seeks and is given foreknowledge of events, as in the case of the Duchess of Gloucester and her hired necromancer, it is useless as a means of preventing disaster, otherwise, of course, it would not be genuinely prophetic.

These implications are worked out far more fully and profoundly in *Macbeth* where, as Wilbur Sanders says, 'there is a sense in which Macbeth has conferred on the prophecy all the reality it possesses, and another sense in which he is the slave of the prophecy'.[7] It seems likely that in this later play Shakespeare consciously pursued the implications of the prophecies he had dramatised in the English histories and *Julius Caesar*, for Macbeth is actually encouraged by the witches' predictions to hasten needlessly on his preordained career. As he himself conjectures,

> If chance will have me King, why chance may crown me
> Without my stir.   (I iii 143–4)

Yet he does 'stir' to the extent of killing Duncan and Banquo and attempting to destroy Banquo's son. Hence, as Sanders says, the prophecies of the witches create the impression that 'a deterministic net has been cast over the whole action. Yet Macbeth proceeds, with every appearance of freedom, to draw the unnecessary conclusion from the prophecies.'[8] These paradoxes are explored far less deeply in the plays under discussion but they do contribute to a comparable effect, namely that Shakespeare's historical characters co-operate voluntarily in bringing upon themselves the very disasters they would avoid. Appeals to God through prayer are, as I have argued, either ineffective or of doubtful efficacy, but the consultation of spirits, and prophetic warnings such as those of Calphurnia or Cassandra carry, in their contexts, even more disturbing implications for the freedom of the will. Far from helping the characters to accomplish their designs, they reveal them, like Oedipus, to be contributors to their own trage-dies. If, as Bradley and others have argued,[9] this combination of ap-parent freedom and actual determinism contributes significantly to the tragic quality of *Macbeth*, then it can reasonably be said to contribute to the tragic quality of those history plays in which pro-phecy plays a role.

The history plays, as I have argued, contain a series of tragedies of fate or fortune but these tragedies convey a sense of pathos or pathetic irony, absent from the plays usually considered tragedies, since the deaths of the protagonists are deprived of the significance of finality by the larger, continuing movement of history in the context of which these deaths occur. The death of Lear, for example, or that of Othello, carries a dramatic 'weight' because it occurs at the end of a play and appears as the culminating outcome of a struggle to which the whole tragedy has been devoted; it is thus endowed with a sense of human significance as an event worthy of our attention. But the placing of the tragedies of, say, Duke Humphrey or Warwick or Falstaff as mere epi-sodes in a continuous process tends to diminish their significance in the continuum of history while not reducing their significance for the individual protagonist. The forces of destiny which control history, in Shakespeare's presentation of it, are binding on the individual yet impervious to his feelings.

The popular and commonly accepted view of Shakespeare's English history plays supports this conclusion while arguing that the two tetralogies, far from being tragic in their effect, are parts of a single drama which is essentially a divine comedy. Tillyard, who gave currency to this idea,[10] which is still generally accepted,[11] argues that what appears in the plays as the operation of fortune is, if regarded rightly, the work of God's providence. He took, in fact, the attitude towards fortune recommended by Boethius, without apparently rea-lising it. Towards the end of the *Consolation* the author contemplates with dismay a world in which joy and sorrow are distributed indiscri-minately to the wicked and the good, and he wonders how he can re-concile such palpable injustices with his belief in a providential deity. He is told by the character of Philosophy,

It is no wonder . . . that a situation should seem random and con-fused when its principle of order is not understood. But, although you do not know why things are as they are, still you cannot doubt that in a world ruled by a good Governor all things do happen justly. . . . . Thus Providence is the unfolding of temporal events as this is present to the vision of the divine mind; but this same unfolding of events as it is worked out in time is called Fate.[12]

Boethius believes that what we experience as fate is actually the manifestation of providence, but, like any orthodox Christian, he does not presume to understand the purposes of providence; he simply asks us to accept in faith that they exist as part of the divine will. Tillyard, and his countless followers, however, argue that Shakespeare thought he did understand God's providential plan for England and that this was the systematic and prolonged punishment of the nation for the dethronement and murder of Richard II, a penitential process completed only on the accession of Richmond, God's chosen agent. This idea is said to have been adopted by Shakespeare from the Tudor historians, particularly Hall, whose chronicle was the main source at least of the three earliest history plays:

> In the total sequence of plays dealing with the subject matter of Hall he expressed successfully a universally held and still comprehensible scheme of history: a scheme fundamentally religious by which events evolve under a law of justice and under the ruling of God's Providence, and of which Elizabeth's England was the acknowledged outcome.[13]

The first thing to be said about this providential interpretation of history is that it was not universally held. As we might expect, there was as much diversity of opinion about religious and political matters in Elizabethan England as there is today, and Shakespeare could find conflicting opinions in the various sources he consulted about the rulers he portrayed. H. A. Kelly has demonstrated in the fullest detail that there was not simply a 'generally accepted' 'Tudor myth' of history to which Shakespeare and his predecessors subscribed, but rival Lancastrian, anti-Lancastrian and Yorkist myths which variously depicted Bolingbroke, Richard II, Edward IV and Henry Tudor either as providential agents of God or as violators of God's purposes for England.[14] According to Thomas Walsingham, for example, Richard II was a corrupt king providentially overthrown by Bolingbroke, whereas according to Hardyng Richard was God's instrument, sinfully murdered by the usurper. 'The establishment of the three royal houses that reigned in England in the fifteenth century, those of Lancaster, York and Tudor, gave rise to a corresponding "myth",[15] and each historian tended, naturally, to favour whichever monarch was in power at the time he wrote or on whose patronage he depended. A more important objection to Tillyard's thesis is that Shakespeare could not find a consistently providential view of history in Hall, supposedly the main proponent of it. Both Hall and Holinshed, as Kelly shows, indiscriminately incorporated the conflicting interpretations of the Lancastrian, Yorkist and Tudor historians on whom they depended for their information with the result that, in their accounts, God's activities in English history are extremely inconsistent.[16] Moreover, when Hall ventures to reveal his own opinions, he is sceptical of all providential theories and actually ridicules such beliefs, as in his account of the troubles which followed the marriage of Edward IV:

> By this marriage, the quenes blood was confounded and utterly in maner destroyed. So that men did afterward divyne, that either God was not contented, nor yet pleased with this matrimony, or els that he punished Kyng Edward in his posteritie, for the diepe dissimulynge and covert clokynge with his faithfull frende the erle of Warwycke. *But such coniectures for the most part, be rather more of mens phantasies, then of divine revelacion* [my italics].[17]

The providential view of the divine purpose behind the troubles of Henry VI's reign is treated with only slightly less scepticism by the supposed originator of it:

> *Other there be that ascribe his infortunitie onely to the stroke and punishment of God,* afferming that the Kingdome, whiche Henry the iiij hys grandfather wrongfully gat, and uniustly possessed agaynst Kyng Richard the ii & his heyres could not by very divyne iustice, longe continew in that iniurious stocke: And that therefore God by his divine providence, punished the offence of the grandfather, in the sonnes son [my italics].[18]

The unavoidable implication is that Hall himself does not subscribe to this view. In a recent study of the Tudor historians, F. J. Levy quotes the following urbane comment by Hall on those who attributed the peace agreement between France and England to the work of God:

This peace was said to be made, onely by the holy ghoste, because
that on the day of metying, a white dove satte on the very toppe of
the kyng of Englandes tent: whether she sat there to drie her, or
came thether as a token, geven by God, I referre it to your judge-
mente.

As Levy rightly remarks 'Hall's emphasis is on the uncertainty of fortune. The divine justice of God provided one form of causation, but
there were times when it seemed inadequate, at least in the sense that
man had no understanding of why God behaved as he did.'[19]

It is hard to agree with Tillyard's belief that the providential
scheme is 'still comprehensible' or, indeed, could have been accept-
able to any but the most naïve Christian since it provokes so many
simple and obvious objections, such as why the disorders of Henry
IV's reign were not sufficient to satisfy God's appetite for justice, why
Henry V's triumphs were allowed to interrupt the nation's course of
penitential suffering and why the innocent and devout Henry VI
should be plagued with its resumption. Tillyard was ready for these
objections:

What were the sins God sought to punish? There had been a number but the pre-eminent one was the murder of Richard II . . .
Henry IV had been punished by an uneasy reign but had not fully
expiated the crime; Henry V, for his piety, had been allowed a bril-
liant reign. But the curse was there; and first England suffers
through Henry V's early death and secondly she is tried by the
witchcraft of Joan.[20]

One wonders why, for his greater piety, Henry VI was not allowed to
live in peace and why nobody in *Henry VI Part I* attributes Henry V's
death to God's avenging providence. Lily B. Campbell, who indepen-
dently reached conclusions not unlike Tillyard's, has a more ingeni-
ous answer to these objections which she discovered not in
Shakespeare's text but in Raleigh's *History of the World*. God's vengeance, in Raleigh's view, never takes effect immediately after a crime
has been committed, but is felt by the grandchild of the offender:

Raleigh . . . took pains in his preface to review English history and
to point out the repetition of the historical pattern which began
with a seizing of the throne and which ended with its loss by the

third heir or the third generation. The throne that Edward III gained, his grandson Richard II lost; the throne that Henry IV gained, his grandson, Henry VI lost; the throne that Edward IV gained, the third heir lost; the throne that Henry VII gained, passed from the Tudors with the death of his grandchild Elizabeth.[21]

(Raleigh was not, incidentally, the originator of this theory, which had been current at least a century earlier.)[22] Professor Campbell's reading of the signs differs significantly from Tillyard's in that, according to her, Elizabeth was the scapegoat for Henry VII's rebellion whereas, according to Tillyard, Elizabeth reaped the harvest of Henry VII's crusade. Both theories read like attempts to crack an unusually difficult code set by the Almighty in order to perplex his creatures.

But even if Hall were a thoroughgoing providentialist, which he is obviously not, and even if Shakespeare consulted no other source, and we know he consulted many, we do a disservice to a writer of the highest genius to attribute to him beliefs of such naïvety. The history plays depict no pattern of sin and divine retribution but display a baffling world from which God's will is concealed. The events portrayed in them do not appear providential but arbitrary and frequently unjust: the pious idealist Henry VI is tormented, the child victims of Richard III are destroyed and the murderess Margaret of Anjou is spared. To this extent the history plays resemble *Titus Andronicus* and *King Lear* and it is hard to believe that Shakespeare paused between the writing of these tragedies and assumed an 'official' face. Moreover he is not so olympian in his vision of the large movements of history as to ignore the private hopes and pains of the individuals involved in them; on the contrary it is his strength to portray their feelings in intimately personal terms:

If the cause be not good, the King himself hath a heavy reckoning to make when all those legs and arms and heads, chopp'd off in a battle, shall join together at the latter day and cry all 'We died at such a place' – some swearing, some crying for a surgeon, some upon their wives left poor behind them, some upon the debts they owe, some upon their children rawly left. I am afeard there are few die well that die in a battle. (*Henry V,* IV i 133–9)

It would be small consolation to the soldiers who died at Agincourt or to the father who killed his son at Towton to know that they were assisting in a providential plan for England. These plays, as I have tried to show, are conceived in terms of individuals struggling to fulfil themselves and Shakespeare's vision is very often one of family relationships – of Priam and his sons debating the state of the Trojan War, of Talbot, like Lear, bearing the body of his dead child, of Edward IV's Queen bewailing the slaughter of her children, of Henry IV apprehensive about his son's succession. If the English histories in their entirety exhibit a total pattern of any kind, and I do not believe that they do, it is a pattern of which an audience in a theatre is not in the least aware. An audience's attention is engaged in the plights of individuals.

This is not, of course, to say that Shakespeare ignores long-term historical causes and effects. Whatever may have been the rights and wrongs of Bolingbroke's seizure of the crown or the conspirators' murder of Julius Caesar or Paris's rape of Helen, their consequences reached out beyond those imagined by their instigators – and, as usually happens in these plays, were not at all in accordance with their expectations. The rebellion by the Percy family against Henry IV broke out as a direct consequence of the deposition and murder of Richard II, but the plays which portray these events provide no certain evidence that civil war was prompted by divine instigation. Each character accounts for the rebellion in accordance with his own personality and sees only such evidence as he is temperamentally inclined to see. The 'providential' interpretation is voiced by the Bishop of Carlisle who, as a churchman and a loyal subject, would be expected to think in this way. For him the deposition is not merely an act of rebellion by subjects against a ruler but a violation of God's representative on earth, 'the figure of God's majesty, His captain, steward, deputy elect, anointed, crowned, planted many years', and national catastrophe must inevitably follow. The Bishop's point of view is the one taken by Tillyard but Shakespeare allows other characters to explain events quite differently. For Henry Bolingbroke the causes of the rebellion are the natural and instinctive grudges felt towards him by those who have helped him to success and were formerly his equals. His analysis of the rebels' motives is entirely consistent with their conduct as Shakespeare portrays it:

[The crown] seem'd in me

But as an honour snatch'd with boist'rous hand;
And I had many living to upbraid
My gain of it by their assistances;
Which daily grew to quarrel and to bloodshed,
Wounding supposed peace.　(*2 Henry IV*, iv v 191–6)

The effects of Richard's murder are also felt during the reign of Henry VI because his death opened up the Yorkist title to the throne and was therefore a major cause of the Wars of the Roses. Significantly it is mentioned only once in *Henry VI Part I* and in that specific context; had Shakespeare held the providential views attributed to him, he would presumably have given some prominence in that play to the sin which the characters are supposed to be expiating. As Hall and Shakespeare both realised, men invoke the idea of providence, as they invoke the idea of fortune, when they try to make sense out of the baffling ways of the world. The plays themselves (as distinct from the characters in them) express the belief – which we have also seen in Machiavelli – that injustice, calamity and frustration are a normal state of affairs and that their ultimate causes lie beyond our comprehension.

So far I have attempted to discover Shakespeare's assumptions about the roles of fortune and providence in history almost entirely on the evidence of the plays themselves and have not considered whether or not his point of view was characteristic of his time. It is, of course, risky to make any generalisations about an age as enquiring and sophisticated in theological matters as that of Elizabeth, but it can at least be said that Shakespeare was not isolated in his belief that the ways of the world were chaotic and often unjust, and that man was so alienated from God that he was incapable of knowing his intentions. We have already seen expressions of this belief in a work which was highly influential in the Middle Ages and the Renaissance, Boethius's *The Consolation of Philosophy*, which was readily available to Shakespeare in its original Latin (and included among its translators both Chaucer and Queen Elizabeth). It was also expressed in another work whose influence was fundamental to Christian theology, Saint Augustine's *The City of God*. There, Augustine makes an absolute distinction between the enduring and deserved rewards which the righteous will enjoy in heaven and the impossibility of true justice in any kingdom of men. In that heavenly city, the Being of God will be

revealed to us, but on earth God's purposes are beyond our understanding:

> We know not why God makes this bad man rich and that good man
> poor; why he should have joy, whose deserts we hold worthier of
> pains, and he pains whose good life we imagine to merit content;
> why the judge's corruption or the falsehood of the witnesses should
> send the innocent away condemned, and the injurious foe should
> depart revenged, as well as unpunished; why the wicked man
> should live sound, and the godly lie bedrid; . . . why infants, of good
> use in the world, should be cut off by untimely death, while they
> that seem unworthy ever to have been born attain long and happy
> life.[23]

A scholar's recent comments on Augustine's view of the state read re-
markably like an observation on the societies portrayed in the history
plays:

> The condition of man consequent on Adam's fall does not allow for
> the achievement of the harmony and order in which alone man can
> find rest. Tension, strife and disorder are endemic in this realm.
> There can be no resolution except eschatologically. Human society
> is irremediably rooted in this tension-ridden and disordered *saecu-
> lum*.[24]

He goes on to say that 'it was this radically "tragic" character of existence for which ancient philosophy, in Augustine's view, could find no
room'.

Whether or not Shakespeare was acquainted with Augustine's
work directly (and the likelihood is that he was not), he could have
become familiar with his thinking indirectly through Calvin and the
Calvinist theologians and preachers of his own day. In a crucial passage in the *Institutes of the Christian Religion*, Calvin argues that our 'slug-
gish minds' are placed 'so far beneath the height of Divine Providence'
that we are unable to comprehend it, with the result that, since the
'order, method, end and necessity of events are, for the most part,
hidden in the counsel of God', they have the appearance of being
fortuitous, 'such being the form under which they present themselves
to us'.[25] He goes on to declare, with a simile which recalls *King Lear*
(and *The Duchess of Malfi*):

As the causes of events are concealed, the thought is apt to rise, that human affairs are whirled about by the blind impulse of Fortune, or our carnal nature inclines us to speak as if God were tossing men up and down like balls.[26]

Calvin does not, of course, believe that the world is ruled by fortune but he acknowledges that events must appear fortuitous because their real purpose is beyond our reach. This was also the view of those theologians who came under the influence of Calvin towards the end of the sixteenth century. It is copiously set out in *An Exposition of the Symbole or Creed of the Apostles* published in 1595 by the much-admired William Perkins, Fellow of Christ's College, Cambridge, and a popular preacher among the students and townspeople of that city. He devotes a substantial section of his commentary to the doctrine of God's providence and the challenges which may be raised against it, among which he includes the objections that 'in the world there is nothing but disorder and confusion, in seditions, treasons, conspiracies and subversions of kingdomes', and that 'with ungodly and wicked men all things go well, and contrawise with the godly all things go hardly'.[27] Perkins does not deny these unpleasant facts – which, incidentally, he attributes to the fall of Adam – but he assures his readers that peace and just rewards will await the righteous in a kingdom other than those of this world. Through his pupils and congregations, Perkins's ideas were disseminated throughout the country, nor was he the only, but merely one of the more celebrated, theologians of Shakespeare's time to be convinced that 'the universe is ruled by an inscrutable God, whose will does not bear impious examination, and will not yield its intent or entertain the speculation of men'.[28] We may possibly have to search no further for the source of Shakespeare's 'agnostic' view of history than the pulpit of the church at Stratford-on-Avon.

Nevertheless I suggested in the previous chapter that the history plays, especially from *Richard II* onwards, do communicate to an audience the sense of a destiny, however incomprehensible, which frustrates his characters of their hopes and even, at times, assists them in hastening their own dooms. We are now perhaps in a better position to understand its real nature. The writers of the Middle Ages thought of it as a goddess with a wheel standing on a rotating ball. Shakespeare uses this image but often mockingly as though he realises that it has become a primitive way of accounting for bad luck, as in Pistol's account of the fate of his companion Bardolph:

> Bardolph, a soldier, firm and sound of heart,
> And of buxom valour, hath by cruel fate
> And giddy Fortune's furious, fickle wheel,
> That goddess blind,
> That stands upon the rolling restless stone –
>
> (*Henry V*, III vi 24–8)

Bardolph, however, is actually about to be hanged for robbing a church and is the victim of the law, not of any irrational goddess. In the place of this relatively primitive image of fortune, Shakespeare creates a more mysterious and, to us, more convincing force working through history. It apparently guides his characters to no single or consistent goal and about the most we can say of it is that it acts in opposition to their wills. I suggest that, just as Shakespeare's characters tend to create a god in the shape of their own wishes, so Shakespeare creates in the force of destiny the embodiment of man's shortcomings and inadequacies. The tensions and struggles depicted in the plays are not, in other words, between the individual's will and his destiny but between his aspirations and his abilities. This idea is stated in relation to love by Troilus to Cressida in a play which often contains explicit statements of notions which are merely implied in the earlier works:

> This is the monstruosity in love, lady, that the will is infinite, and the execution confined; that the desire is boundless, and the act a slave to limit.   *Troilus and Cressida*, III ii 77–80)

There is clearly a similarity between Troilus's complaint here and Agamemnon's more metaphorical observation on war:

> checks and disasters
> Grow in the veins of actions highest rear'd,
> As knots, by the conflux of meeting sap,
> Infect the sound pine, and divert his grain
> Tortive and errant from his course of growth.
>
> (I iii 5–9)

Piety is a feeble resource in the struggle against destiny – otherwise Henry VI would have been a successful politician – but intelligence and self-knowledge are of value, as Henry V demonstrates. Perhaps all I am saying is that the characters who have least cause to blame their destiny are those who are best equipped to create it for themselves, but Shakespeare is not guilty of this truism. What he does make us realise is the difficulty of surviving in a world as complex as our own when our equipment for survival is so flawed and inadequate, and that brings us back to the Fall and its consequences. Instead of the providential interpretation of the histories, I prefer to apply to them Schopenhauer's comment on tragedy, which he sees as issuing from the nature of man itself:

> The scornful mastery of chance, and the irretrievable fall of the just and innocent, is here presented to us; and in this lies a significant hint of the nature of the world and of existence. It is the strife of will with itself, which here, completely unfolded at the highest grade of its objectivity, comes into fearful prominence . . . The demand for so-called poetical justice rests on an entire misconception of the nature of tragedy and, indeed, the nature of the world itself . . . But only the dull, optimistic, Protestant-rationalistic, or peculiarly Jewish view of life will make the demand for poetical justice, and find satisfaction in it. The true sense of tragedy is the deeper insight, that it is not his own individual sins that the hero atones for, but original sin, *i.e.* the crime of existence itself.[29]

All the human insufficiencies that are accounted for in the myth of the Fall – the ignorance, the miscalculation, the misunderstanding of ourselves and others, the effects of age and death – are gathered together in the powerfully numinous presence of destiny, and it is this presence which gives to the history plays their weight, their excitement and their tragic potential. Yet the impression I am creating that the history plays are mournful, depressing works, is also wrong: Schopenhauer's later idea that tragedy induces us to turn away from life with a sad resignation[30] obviously does not apply to, say, *Henry IV Part I* and a good deal of *Henry V*. The histories are also full of abundant and zestful life, in such figures as Jack Cade, Richard of Gloucester and particularly Falstaff. What prevents these plays from creating the impression that 'life can afford us no true pleasure'[31] is the stubborn vitality with which such people set about the impossible task of shaping their destinies. 'Give me life!', says the ageing Falstaff: his demand is at the same time exhilarating and pathetic.

5 | *Knowledge and Judgement*

The episode in Glendower's castle in *Henry IV Part I* gives a fresh interest to the midde of the play by introducing a vividly eccentric new character. It also introduces a different kind of comedy from that of the tavern scenes, created by the incompatibility of Glendower and Hotspur. Their temperamental differences are obvious from the moment when the leaders sit down to their conference: Hotspur ridicules Glendower's claim that his birth was accompanied by supernatural portents, and when Glendower reveals that he was once a poet, Hotspur derides the whole art of poetry. For all his chivalric idealism, Hotspur's contempt is that of a rationalist for a romantic and, during Glendower's absence from the conference table, he confides to Mortimer how much the Welshman infuriates him:

> O, he is as tedious
> As a tired horse, a railing wife;
> Worse than a smoky house; I had rather live
> With cheese and garlic in a windmill, far,
> Than feed on cates and have him talk to me
> In any summer house in Christendom.   (III i 159–64)

Mortimer, however, has a quite different opinion of his father-in-law and he tactfully protests that Glendower is learned, courageous, 'wondrous affable' and, moreover, has the highest regard for Hotspur. The two opinions are not inconsistent but, since Glendower appears only in this one scene, we have no means of knowing which estimate is the more just, though one suspects Hotspur of prejudice: it is the penalty he pays for having such a vital personality of his own.

These conflicting opinions and partial judgements are typical of *Henry IV*; indeed the action of many of Shakespeare's plays depends on the fact that our knowledge of other people must necessarily be not absolute but subjective, and that it is impossible for one man totally to know another. The consequences can be amusing, as in the clashes between Hotspur and Glendower, or tragic as in Othello's misconception of Desdemona. The absurdities of *The Comedy of Errors* derive from the belief by most of the characters that, because one man looks like another, he must necessarily be another, and the agonies of Lear derive from his assumption that his daughters really mean what they say.

No doubt Shakespeare observed as a fact of life that our estimates of one another are subjective, contradictory and unreliable. That it is a fact of life and should not be so is another implication of the myth of the fall of Adam, for it was a commonly held belief that in his primal innocence Adam had perfect knowledge and judgement, the evidence for which was his ability to give names to all the creatures God had made. As Milton puts it,

> *Adam* who had the wisdom giv'n him to know all creatures, and to name them according to their properties, no doubt but had the gift to discern perfectly, that which concern'd him much more; and to apprehend at first sight the true fitnes of that consort which God provided him.[1]

This situation, in which everything appears to be what it actually is, was permanently disrupted by the deceptions imposed by Satan on Eve, as a consequence of which, as Isabel MacCaffrey says,

> the deceitfulness of things makes life a struggle, a hill to be laboured up, a maze of pitfalls, a mass of confusions to be 'culled out and sorted asunder'. Whitehead has defined truth as 'the conformation of Appearance to Reality'; after Satan's rebellion and man's sin the two are no longer congruent.[2]

Donne gives an exhilarating account of the ease with which the souls of the righteous in heaven will have access to all knowledge, not passing 'from Author to Author as in a Grammar School, nor from Art to Art as in an University; but as that General which Knighted his whole Army, God shall create us Doctors in a minute'.[3] Whereas in that heavenly paradise we shall regain the perfect knowledge and discernment once possessed by Adam in the earthly paradise, we are now compelled to rely on impressions and conjectures which seldom correspond with reality. Though Shakespeare no doubt saw false perceptions and errors of judgement in the world around him, the Genesis story, as interpreted theologically, provided an explanation for them: 'our very eyes are, sometimes, like our judgements, blind' (*Cymbeline*, IV ii 302–3).

This uneasy sense of the fallibility of our perceptions, the disabling conviction that we can have no certain knowledge either of the physical world or of the people among whom we move, was not felt exclusively by Shakespeare in his own time. It was a major preoccupation of renaissance thinkers, partly under the influence of Calvin, whose theology emphasised the inadequacies of man's fallen intellect, partly because of a renewed interest in ancient Greek scepticism, particularly that of Sextus Empiricus whose philosophical treatise *The Pyrrhonic Hypotyposes* was published in a new Latin translation by Henri Estienne in 1562.[4] Sir Walter Raleigh's fragmentary essay *The Sceptick*, posthumously published in 1651, was, incidentally, an almost literal translation of part of the *Hypotyposes*. By far the greatest and most influential expression of scepticism in the Renaissance was, however, the *Essays* of Montaigne which Shakespeare certainly read in the English translation of John Florio (see below, p. 127). Although Florio's version did not appear in print before 1603, when the dramatist was more or less half-way through his professional career, Shakespeare may, nevertheless, have become acquainted with it before then, for it is known to have circulated widely in manuscript. Moreover both writers enjoyed the favours of the same two patrons, the Earl of Southampton and the Earl of Pembroke.[5] The translator and the playwright could well have been acquaintances, if not friends.

This revived preoccupation with philosophical scepticism, with the belief that our sense-impressions may be deceptive, is also to be found in the pleas made by Bacon that his readers should rid themselves of popular superstitions, unquestioning acceptance of received opinions and personal prejudices which may have no relation to reality. Our natural prejudices, Bacon argued, induce us to worship what he termed the 'Idols of the Cave' which he described in a celebrated passage of his *Novum Organum* (1620):

The Idols of the Cave are the idols of the individual man. For every one (besides the errors common to human nature in general) has a cave or den of his own, which refracts and discolours the light of nature; owing either to his own proper and peculiar nature; or to his education and conversation with others; or to the reading of books, and the authority of those he esteems and admires; or to the differences of impression, accordingly as they take place in a mind preoccupied and predisposed or in a mind indifferent and settled; or the like. So that the spirit of man (according as it is meted out to different individuals) is in fact a thing variable and full of perturbation, and governed as it were by chance.[6]

This difference between what the literary critics usually call 'illusion and reality', which preoccupied Shakespeare throughout his entire life as a dramatist, was very much a concern of his immediate contemporaries.

The role of the King, as it is portrayed in the early scenes of *Richard II*, allows him to control his subjects in accordance with his own will, making war or peace, settling disputes among his peers, and levying money from his people to carry out his policies. The respect which his subjects accord him, of the kind which is voiced in the fulsome words of Mowbray and Bolingbroke in the opening lines, tends to reinforce the King's conviction that he is the centre of his world and that his subjects exist largely in order to carry out his wishes. Richard, in the first two acts of the play, shows the tendency which has preoccupied the existentialist philosophers 'to reduce our world to order, to manage it for our own ends, to control it for our own particular purposes'.[7] When Mowbray and Bolingbroke refuse to be managed as the King wishes by not agreeing to bury their quarrel, Richard still has the authority to prevent their interference in his world by banishing them from it. The King is, however, circumscribed by certain traditionally respected laws which prevent him from exercising absolute control over his subjects, and when he seizes for his own purposes the lands and wealth to which Bolingbroke is entitled on the death of his father, Richard oversteps the boundaries which traditionally define the limits of his authority. As York protests,

> Take Hereford's rights away, and take from Time
> His charters and his customary rights,
> Let not tomorrow then ensue today;
> Be not thyself – for how art thou a king
> But by fair sequence and succession?   (II i 195–9)

In existentialist terms, Richard's seizure of Bolingbroke's inheritance is an example of our tendency to 'treat other people as things, for if they were things, if they lost their power to act, we should at least be able to exercise a reasonable degree of control over them'.[8] But Bolingbroke, very reasonably, refuses to be treated as a mere chattel in Richard's world and, knowing that traditional rights are on his side, returns to demand the property which is his due. By the time Richard returns from Ireland, he begins to realise that whereas formerly Bolingbroke existed largely as a component in his world, now he himself is in danger of being reduced to the role of a component in Bolingbroke's world. In Sartre's words, 'By the mere appearance of the Other, I am put in the position of passing judgement on myself as on an object, for it is as an object that I appear to the Other.'[9] It is this discovery that accounts for Richard's violent oscillations between over-confidence and complete despair in the scene (III ii) where the truth dawns on him. He changes back and forth between a vision of himself as king, supported in his imagination by a conscience-stricken and repentant Bolingbroke and an army of heavenly angels, and a vision of himself as a man indistinguishable from any other:

> I live with bread like you, feel want,
> Taste grief, need friends; subjected thus,
> How can you say to me I am a king?　(III ii 175–7)

Richard's pun emphasises the inward nature of his discovery: he is 'subjected' to the power of Bolingbroke's soldiers, but he also sees himself as a mere subject in a world centred on Bolingbroke.

The discrepancy between their two views of themselves and their worlds appears very strongly in the deposition scene which each man, very naturally, interprets in accordance with what he believes to be his role in it.[10] For Bolingbroke the transfer of the crown is a public ceremony of abdication, necessary to legitimise the transfer of power:

> Fetch hither Richard, that in common view
> He may surrender; so we shall proceed
> Without suspicion.　(IV i 155–7)

For Richard, on the other hand, the ceremony is one of usurpation, a public demonstration that he is being forcibly dethroned. Each man has, as it were, written his own scenario for the performance and is determined that his version is the one that will be played. The difference between the two versions extends to the language and gestures which each insists should be used. Richard instructs Bolingbroke as a director instructs a principal actor:

> Give me the crown. Here, cousin, seize the crown.

In turn, Bolingbroke tries to instruct Richard whom he regards as an actor in the play he has created:

> Are you contented to resign the crown?

But, though Richard finally does agree to 'resign', he refuses to play the rest of the scene Bolingbroke has written for him and to confess to the list of crimes drawn up against him; indeed, he sees as mere 'follies' those actions which Northumberland regards as 'grievous crimes'. As a parting gesture, he turns Bolingbroke's irritated dismissal of him against the usurper and shows the performance to be what he, Richard, thinks it is:

> BOLINGBROKE   Go, some of you, convey him to the Tower.
> RICHARD   O, good! Convey! Conveyers are you all
> That rise thus nimbly by a true king's fall.   (iv i 316–18)

In prison, however, he fails to discover his true identity, unable to accept himself either as essentially a king or as a common subject. Before his death he seems, in his own mind, to have no identity, to be nothing but an idea in the mind of Bolingbroke, a clock which measures his rise to power (v v 49–60). His Barbary horse, he hears, is now proud to carry the usurper, and is content to be a portion of Bolingbroke's world as it once was of Richard's. The fallen monarch's state of mind during his last moments is illuminated, rather unexpectedly, by an observation made by Bacon in his essay 'Of Truth'. 'Doth any man doubt', he remarks,

> that if there were taken out of men's minds vain opinions, flattering hopes, false valuations, imaginations as one would, and the like, but it would leave the minds of a number of men poor shrunken things, full of melancholy and indisposition, and unpleasing to themselves?[11]

By this stage in his career Shakespeare had become interested in man as 'a "reflective" being: self-picturing self-deceiving, and acutely aware of the regard of others', as Iris Murdoch says of Sartre's view of human nature.[12] The inescapable tendency of men to create their own world-views, to see themselves and others not in absolute, objective terms but subjectively according to their own characters and situations was dramatised fully by Shakespeare for the first time in *Richard II*. The conflict between different ways of perceiving the same situation put him in mind of the kind of pictures known as 'perspectives', which are painted on a corrugated surface and present different subjects depending on whether they are viewed from the left or the right, but looked at from the front appear confused. This is used metaphorically by Bushy in his attempt to console the Queen:

> Each substance of a grief hath twenty shadows,
> Which shows like grief itself, but is not so;
> For sorrow's eye, glazed with blinding tears,
> Divides one thing entire to many objects,
> Like perspectives which, rightly gaz'd upon,
> Show nothing but confusion – ey'd awry,
> Distinguish form. So your sweet Majesty,
> Looking awry upon your lord's departure,
> Find shapes of grief more than himself to wail;
> Which, look'd on as it is, is nought but shadows
> Of what it is not.   (II ii 14–24)

As things turn out it is, of course, Bushy who perceives things mistakenly. In this play men are not deceived by appearances, like the characters in *The Comedy of Errors*, but instinctively create a world of appearances with which to surround themselves. It is therefore difficult to decide which is the 'correct', objective version of the events which the play portrays. We are left to weigh up at least two conflicting versions, Richard's and Bolingbroke's, and form our own opinion; the plays which succeed it, the two parts of *Henry IV*, contain yet more versions of the deposition as it was seen by Worcester, Hotspur, and Henry in his later years. This mode of presentation also allows Shakespeare to incorporate into the play the conflicting interpretations of the historians, for Richard is seen within the play both as an incompetent tyrant (Northumberland's view) and as a royal martyr (Richard's view of himself). As H. A. Kelly has shown, some of the characters give a 'Lancastrian' and others a 'Yorkist' version of events within the same play.[13] (See page 68 above.) Shakespeare seems to have realised that our inability to perceive absolute truth extends to our judgement of the dead: his view of history includes the idea that we can never know what history really consists of.

The irreconcilable conflict between people's individual conceptions of one another is also a feature of the comedies and is fully developed in *The Merchant of Venice*, a play written about a year after *Richard II*. In the figure of Shylock Shakespeare created a character who was to become controversial for this very reason. A member of an unjustly persecuted race in his own eyes, and a predatory monster in the eyes of people like Gratiano, he voices his own subjective impression of the play so eloquently that, since the beginning of the eighteenth century, the critics have been in constant disagreement as to whether his or the Christians' is the authentic version: the play is a tragedy or a comedy depending on whether you see it through Shylock's eyes or those of the Christians.* Shylock is obviously the most vital and imposing character in this play, but Shakespeare's next history play, *Henry IV Part I*, abounds with independent, idiosyncratic, energetic characters such as Hotspur, Falstaff, Hal, the King, and a host of vividly realised minor people, all reluctant to be governed, tending to see the world in their own terms and to dictate their terms to other people. The play has scarcely begun before there is a clash of wills between the King and Hotspur which takes the form of an argument about the true character and conduct of Mortimer. To Henry, Mortimer is a traitor who has betrayed his troops to the enemy; to Hotspur, Mortimer is a loyal subject who has proved his faithfulness in violent combat against Glendower. Henry's reaction to Hotspur's report of this encounter is to call him a liar, and Hotspur's reaction is to accuse Henry of misrepresenting the truth for his own purposes, for Mortimer has a strong claim to the throne. Neither allows the other to be right, and their disagreement, incidentally, allows Shakespeare to incorporate into his play the uncertainty he found in Holinshed, who wrote that 'whether by treason or otherwise . . . the English power was discomfited, the

---

* In his *Account of the Life of Mr. William Shakespeare*, (1709), Nicholas Rowe remarks: 'Tho' we have seen that Play Receiv'd and Acted as a Comedy, and the Part of the *Jew* perform'd by an Excellent Comedian, yet I cannot but think it was design'd Tragically by the Author' (Shakespeare, *Works*, 6 vols (London, 1709) vol. I, pp. xix–xx.

earle taken prisoner, and above a thousand of his people slaine in the place'.[14] What actually happened we can never know: the mild, affable man who appears later in the play seems neither treacherous nor a warrior. It should be noticed, however, that the row over Mortimer helps to spark off the Percys' rebellion: it propels Hotspur into the arms of his already mutinous uncle and we must conclude that the impulse which encouraged Hotspur to ally himself with the rebels resulted from a possible misjudgement of the facts.

We have already noticed the tendency of Bolingbroke and Richard to regard each other as objects in their own subjective worlds, but the action of *Henry IV* is distributed between different physical worlds or locations, each dominated by a unique and uniquely demanding character. The court is dominated by Henry, solitary and obsessed with affairs of state, the tavern by Falstaff, gregarious and devoted to the satisfaction of his appetites, and the rebel camp by Hotspur, independent and preoccupied by the desire for fame in battle. Each world is vividly real but is also an image of the character who dominates it (in a manner reminiscent of the 'houses' of medieval allegory) and each of the major protagonists sees the others subjectively as aids or impediments to the achievement of success within his own individual world. There is, in particular, a wide variety of opinion about Prince Hal who plays a crucial role in all three worlds. To Hotspur, Hal is a mere playboy, 'the sword and buckler Prince of Wales', but also, however trivial, a threat to his ambition to be the unrivalled champion of chivalry. As he dies on the battlefield, Hotspur is galled to think that, far from winning honour by the defeat of Hal, he has actually contributed to Hal's reputation by falling at his hands:

> I better brook the loss of brittle life
> Than those proud titles thou has won of me:
> They wound my thoughts worse than thy sword my flesh.
>
> (v iv 78–80)

Whereas Hotspur regards the Prince as a threat to his reputation and is nettled by Vernon's eulogy of him, the King fears Hal as a threat to the succession and the stability of the country to which he has laboriously devoted his reign. In Henry's eyes, Hal is a dangerous profligate whose accession will initiate a further period of political chaos, whereas Hotspur is an ideal son whose character and achievements overshadow Hal's. Hotspur, as Henry tells his son,

hath more worthy interest to the state
Than thou the shadow of succession.   (*1 Henry IV*, III ii 98–9)

In spite of Hal's display of loyalty at the Battle of Shrewsbury, the King, almost up to the moment of his death, continues to see his son as a danger to the state. When Hal, towards the end of the *Second Part*, moved by the thought of the immense responsibilities he is about to assume, takes the crown from his father's pillow, Henry interprets his gesture as a confirmation of his worst suspicions about his son:

> Thou hast stol'n that which, after some few hours,
> Were thine without offence; and at my death
> Thou hast seal'd up my expectation.
> Thy life did manifest thou lov'dst me not,
> And thou wilt have me die assur'd of it.
>
> (*2 Henry IV*, IV v 102–6)

To the King, Hal is a character in his own tragedy.

Falstaff shares with Hotspur and the King the impression that Hal is a profligate, and, in spite of the Prince's continual protests to the contrary, persists in seeing him as a lifelong ally in crime. Whereas Henry foresees Hal's accession as the ruin of his aspirations, Falstaff foresees it as the realisation of his hopes, and he rides off to London convinced that the young King is sick for him. To each of these three people, Hal is a character in his own private drama, a subjective impression created in his own mind. Each regards him as a creature to be used. It does not, apparently, occur to any of them that Hal may be using them. The Prince shares this secret only with the audience who are allowed to learn that his association with Falstaff is a deliberately assumed appearance of profligacy, designed to 'falsify men's hopes' in order that his well-timed public 'reformation' may compel the admiration of his subjects. To his mind he is the sun, the centre of a universe in which Falstaff is not an ally but a mere 'base contagious cloud' which he permits, for the moment, to obscure his own beauty, a 'foil' with which he will eventually dispense (*1 Henry IV*, I ii 188–210). Hal regards Falstaff, as Falstaff regards Hal, as an instrument in his own ascent to power. The rejection scene portrays the inevitable collision of these two views in which Hal's prevails, not because it is the truer but because Hal has the necessary power to enforce it. It is only then

that Falstaff discovers not simply that he has no future but that he is
no more than a disgusting idea in the mind of Henry V:

> I have long dreamt of such a kind of man,
> So surfeit-swell'd, so old and so profane;
> But, being awak'd, I do despise my dream.   (*2 Henry IV*, v v 50–2)

At that moment, Falstaff begins to wake from his dream too.

The lives of all these characters are shown to have been built upon
conjectures which are unavoidable and in most cases lead to disaster.
Hotspur builds his hopes on the illusion that the Prince is a shallow
profligate, easily disposed of, Falstaff on the illusion that Hal's seem-
ing loyalty will ensure his future, and, though the King's fears of Hal
are luckily dispelled just before he dies, nevertheless he wastes the
night hours dreading his son's accession.

The rebellion against Henry is likewise motivated by conjectures.
Worcester, its instigator, simply assumes that the King will continue
to be embarrassed by his former dependence on the Percys, that he
will expect them to trade on this dependence and will therefore find an
excuse to be rid of them:

> For, bear ourselves as even as we can,
> The King will always think him in our debt,
> And think we think ourselves unsatisfied,
> Till he hath found a time to pay us home.
>
> (*1 Henry IV*, i iii 285–8)

It is on this projection of his own fears into what he imagines to be the
mind of Bolingbroke that Worcester initiates the rebellion. Even
when, immediately before the crucial battle, Henry offers them an
amnesty, Worcester is unable to take him at his word:

> It is not possible, it cannot be,
> The King should keep his word in loving us;
> He will suspect us still, and find a time
> To punish this offence in other faults.   (v ii 4–7)

On this conjecture, he deliberately conceals the King's offer of peace
from Hotspur who, as we are later told, leads his men into battle on

the false assumption that his strength will be sufficient to overcome the enemy:

> [He] lin'd himself with hope,
> Eating the air and promise of supply,
> Flatt'ring himself in project of a power
> Much smaller than the smallest of his thoughts;
> And so, with great imagination
> Proper to madmen, led his powers to death
> And, winking, leapt into destruction.   (*2 Henry IV*, I ii 27–33)

Hotspur's death, like the defeat of Falstaff's hopes, is caused by a failure of perception. He misconstrues everything.

One consequence of this tendency to misjudgement is that the characters constantly accuse one another of lying. Henry IV accuses Hotspur and Hotspur accuses the King of lying about Mortimer; the Prince accuses Falstaff of lying about the Gadshill robbery; Worcester refuses to believe in the King's offer of an amnesty and deliberately lies about it to Hotspur; Falstaff claims the credit for killing Hotspur and observes how subject old men like Shallow are to this vice of lying. Appropriately the Second Part of the play is introduced by the figure of Rumour, 'painted full of tongues'. Another manifestation of this subjectivity is the prominence of episodes in which characters impersonate one another: Prince Hal gives an impersonation of breakfast-time at Warkworth which does not quite correspond to the behaviour of Hotspur and his wife which we have witnessed in the previous scene (*1 Henry IV*, II iii), and, although we are denied the promised pleasure of seeing Falstaff play Lady Percy, we do see him, together with Hal, in a charade of the Prince's forthcoming interview with the King. Such mimicry reveals as much about the attitudes of the performers as it does about the characters they impersonate. The winner in this game of deception is Hal, who deliberately impersonates the prodigal son and feigns the false impression he knows his subjects have formed of him in order that, eventually, they will be convinced by his equally contrived reformation. Only he succeeds in an imperfect world by ingeniously exploiting its imperfections. Yet it is doubtful whether Hal himself knows wholly what he is doing: his assurances, in his first soliloquy, that his profligacy is merely a sham, may be an attempt to justify his actions to himself, and his later confession to the Lord Chief Justice that he is a reformed character presupposes that he was formerly corrupt.* Just as we can never be sure of Bolingbroke's motives for returning from exile, we can never absolutely know Hal's motives for frequenting the tavern. The two parts of *Henry IV* are almost as open to our own subjective interpretations as they are to those of the protagonists; hence the continual critical discussion about their 'real' meaning.

We are offered almost as many contradictory opinions of Julius Caesar as we are of Prince Hal. Cassius regards Caesar as a man no better than himself who has already reached a position of tyrannical power. The image he creates of Caesar is one observed from his own inferior position:

> Why, man, he doth bestride the narrow world
> Like a Colossus, and we petty men
> Walk under his huge legs, and peep about
> To find ourselves dishonourable graves.   (ɪ ii 135–8)

He is not satisfied until he bestrides the body of Caesar in the Capitol. Brutus, Caesar's intimate friend, can see no evidence that he has aspirations to dictatorial power:

> To speak truth of Caesar,
> I have not known when his affections sway'd
> More than his reason.   (ɪɪ i 19–21)

His decision to ally himself with the conspirators is based wholly on the conjecture that Caesar 'would be', or wants to be, crowned king, and on the prediction that, once crowned, he might become ruthless. But the play offers no conclusive evidence that this is Caesar's intention. We never witness the critical ceremony on the Lupercal in which a crown is offered to him: it happens off-stage and we have only the conjectures of the sceptical Casca to suggest that he was tempted to accept it:

I saw Mark Antony offer him a crown – yet 'twas not a crown neither, 'twas one of these coronets – and, as I told you, he put it by

---

* This was Johnson's interpretation of the soliloquy, which he described as 'a natural picture of a great mind offering excuses to itself, and palliating those follies which it can neither justify nor forsake'; Arthur Sherbo (ed.), *Johnson on Shakespeare*, 2 vols (Yale edition, 1968) vol. ɪ, p. 458.

once; but for all that, to my thinking he would fain have had it.
Then he offered it to him again; then he put it by again; but to my
thinking he was very loath to lay his fingers off it.   (I ii 238–46)

Vivid though Casca's account is, it both leaves Caesar's intentions in
doubt and, at the same time, reveals Casca as a cynic, a 'blunt fellow',
and not a wholly reliable witness. The other eye-witness, Mark
Antony, places a totally different interpretation on Caesar's gesture of
refusal:

> You all did see that on the Lupercal
> I thrice presented him a kingly crown
> Which he did thrice refuse. Was this ambition?
> Yet Brutus says he was ambitious;
> And sure he is an honourable man.
> I speak not to disprove what Brutus spoke,
> But here I am to speak what I do know.   (III ii 95–101)

We never know the real significance of that gesture which is such a
powerful incentive to the conspirators. Needless to say, Antony deliberately exploits its ambiguity in order to whip up public hostility
against Brutus, but this is no reason to conclude that Antony's opinion is not sincerely held: he has a talent for putting his own deeply felt
feelings at the service of his ambitions. Throughout the first part of the
play we are given totally contradictory judgements of Caesar's character and intentions. The impression we receive from the man himself, during his few appearances, credulous, ageing, sick, arrogant,
but still shrewd and powerfully authoritative, could support any of
these views. His character is vital and complex but, by the time he is
dead, we know him no more absolutely than anyone in the play does.
Shakespeare's presentation of him is what Ernest Schanzer calls 'a
dramatic treatment in the manner of Pirandello. "Which of these is
the real Caesar?" Shakespeare seems to ask. And he takes care not to
provide an answer.'[15]
    The subjective and incompatible impressions which Brutus and
Antony receive of Caesar lead them to conceive of the assassination
itself in conflicting terms. For Brutus it is a dispassionate act, deliberately performed according to high moral principles:

> Let's be sacrificers, but not butchers, Caius.

> . . . And, gentle friends,
> Let's kill him boldly, but not wrathfully;
> Let's carve him as a dish fit for the gods,
> Now hew him as a carcase fit for hounds.   (II i 166; 171–4)

Antony's judgement of the deed is precisely the one Brutus is anxious to dispel:

> O, pardon me, thou bleeding piece of earth,
> That I am meek and gentle with these butchers!   (III i 255–6)

Although Antony persuades the mob, if not in so many words, that Brutus is a liar, there is no reason to suppose that each of them does not sincerely believe in the version of events as he sees it. Their successive orations are attempts to shape the pliable minds of the mob into agreement with their own personal conceptions of history and we should be hard put to decide which, if either, of the two men was deceiving himself. As Schanzer has shown,[16] the professional historians have held divergent opinions about the motives of Caesar, Brutus and Antony almost from the moment when the assassination took place; Shakespeare has incorporated these contrary and subjective judgements into the play and the literary critics are still taking sides. The tragic irony contained in the play is that, just as Hotspur lost his life in a rebellion motivated by conjecture, so Brutus murdered his friend and Antony stirred up a civil mutiny for reasons which were 'true' only in a subjective sense, that is, true in terms of the political situation as they saw it. A further irony is created at the expense of the well-intentioned Brutus in that, according to his projection of events, the murder of Caesar will terminate an oppressive period of Roman history, whereas in Antony's mind the murder is rather the beginning of a period of civil war. Immediately after the assassination, the conspirators conduct themselves as though the whole drama were concluded and they were preparing to make a final exit:

> DECIUS   What, shall we forth?
> CASSIUS   Ay, every man away.
> Brutus shall lead, and we will grace his heels
> With the most boldest and best hearts of Rome.   (III i 120–2)

At this point, however, with the stage direction *'Enter a Servant'*, Shakespeare, with marvellous dramatic tact, demonstrates that, contrary to the expectations of the assassins, the play is merely entering another phase,[17] the phase controlled by Antony in whose mind the conspirators are wilful butchers, and it is Antony's view of recent history which prevails – that is, until he himself becomes an impediment in the mind of the as yet shadowy figure of Octavius. The whole play depends on the tendency whereby 'men may construe things after their fashion, Clean from the purpose of the things themselves' (I iii 34–5).

One reason why *Henry IV* and *Julius Caesar* are greater plays than the early histories is that Shakespeare conveys to his audience with equal vividness and conviction the conflicting impressions of people involved in the historical process. In this respect the plays are more like historical novels than chronicles: Scott was to learn a great deal from them. It is a common critical fallacy to assume that the world as seen by Hal or Falstaff or Brutus or Antony is the world as seen by Shakespeare. The dramatist himself can imagine and communicate all their conflicting impressions but what he himself sees is essentially a series of conflicts, unavoidable because they derive from innate, postlapsarian ignorance. Nearly all the history plays are concerned with war or civil war, but the wars originate not so much from any particular action such as the murder of Richard II or the assassination of Caesar but from the conflicting projections made by individuals upon the world which surrounds them, and, as Sartre argues, these projections upon the world 'include perception of it, feeling things about it, making plans to change it, and intervening in its course'.[18]

The most vivid and powerful vision of the Trojan War is no doubt that of Thersites, but this is because his vision is a very simple, reductive one, tempting to adopt because it requires less attention to the complexities of the characters and their views of one another. In fact the Greek and Trojan leaders do not correspond to the grotesque caricatures Thersites draws of them. Diomedes is not simply a 'dissembling abominable varlet', Troilus is more than a 'scurvy, doting foolish young knave', Cressida is not just a 'dissembling luxurious drab', and Patroclus is not a 'fool positive'. They are generally fallible, limited, erring creatures doing their best in a war which they can neither win nor bring to an end. Thersites's sick version of the story is only one among many. Troilus's sensualist idealisation of Cressida differs from Pandarus's indulgent, sexually pragmatic view of her; and Ulysses's assumption that she is no more than 'sluttish spoils of opportunity' is not wholly substantiated by the impression she herself conveys to us of a half-well-intentioned, shallow, confused girl. Even Cressida herself appears baffled about her character and intentions as she stands half-willing to abandon herself to Troilus and half-reluctant to lose her independence:

> I have a kind of self resides with you;
> But an unkind self, that itself will leave
> To be another's fool. I would be gone.
> Where is my wit? I know not what I speak.   (III ii 144–7)

She is uncertain whether Troilus genuinely loves her or is merely abusing her, but nor does she know whether her own protestations of love are sincere and spontaneous or an unconsciously prepared bait with which to lure her lover:

> Perchance, my lord, I show more craft than love;
> And fell so roundly to a large confession
> To angle for your thoughts; but you are wise –
> Or else you love not; for to be wise and love
> Exceeds man's might.   (III ii 149–53)

These tremulous emotions are those of a young woman confused by the conflicting impressions of adolescence who fails to understand whether she is an object to be used by Troilus or he is an object to be used by her. The most elaborate set of conflicting impressions appears in the episode (v ii) in which Cressida abandons Troilus for Diomedes. Unknown to her and her new lover, the two of them are observed by the worldly-wise Ulysses and by Troilus, who is stunned by her sudden infidelity; unknown to them, the whole scene is watched with perverse relish by Thersites. A. P. Rossiter's comment on the episode is very much to the point:

> Shakespeare makes it utterly clear that for every participant in the scene there is a phenomenon called 'Cressida': Thersites' is no more Ulysses' (though both think her a mere flirt) than Diomed's is Troilus'; nor is Cressida's Cressida like any of these. In each, the individual consciousness spontaneously generates its own norms,

and enjoys complete freedom in 'making its own existence'. But this is the same as showing that there are *no* norms, in the sense in which traditional philosophy assumes them. The absolutes are myths. The supposed 'rule in unity itself' is only a fallacious attempt to stifle my awareness that I am I, and (whichever I may be: Ulysses or Thersites or Troilus) that my 'her' is for me the only 'she'.[19]

The tragic discovery which Troilus makes as he sees Cressida hand over his love-token to Diomedes is comparable to the discoveries made by Richard II in prison and Falstaff on his rejection by the Prince: he discovers that he is an 'object' in the subjective world created by Cressida and is unable to reconcile this vision with his former belief that she was an 'object' faithful to his impression of her. His reaction is to re-enter the battle, vowing revenge on Diomedes. Shakespeare's audience, familiar with the various accounts of his story, no doubt knew that Troilus was killed in the war.

Just as the impressions formed by the characters in *Troilus and Cressida* about one another are subjective and divergent, so are their judgements of a collective enterprise, the Trojan War; it is characteristic of the play that a central scene takes the form of a debate on the nature and value of the whole undertaking. It appears that, at the time Paris abducted Helen, his brothers all thought highly of her, since, as Troilus says, they all 'clapped hands and cried "Inestimable!"'. Now they are well acquainted with her and have made sacrifices on her behalf, Hector has other views: she is, in his opinion, 'a thing not ours', for whom Trojan blood has been spilt, and is inherently 'not worth what she doth cost The keeping' (ii ii 51–2). For Troilus, on the other hand, she is the inspiration for acts of military valour,

> A spur to valiant and magnanimous deeds,
> Whose present courage may beat down our foes,
> And fame in time to come canonize us.   (ii ii 200–2)

For Troilus she is the cause of heroic actions, for Hector the cause of needless bloodshed. This conflict of opinion induces the Trojan leaders to consider the very principles on which judgements are made and whether the absolute reality of an enterprise can be distinguished from the impression received by the mind that observes it. Troilus, without hesitation, asserts that judgements must necessarily be subjective:

What's aught but as 'tis valued?   (II ii 52)

Hector argues, on the other hand, that the value of a thing is not to be found in any personal estimate but that it has an absolute, inherent worth of its own:

> But value dwells not in particular will:
> It holds his estimate and dignity
> As well wherein 'tis precious of itself
> As in the prizer.   (II ii 53–6)

But if such an absolute value exists, it is impossible to see, within the terms offered by the play, how it can be separated from the subjective estimates made by those who perceive it. But as well as observing Hector's and Troilus's (and Paris's and Thersites's) view of Helen, the audience is given, in her single brief appearance, an opportunity to form its own opinion, which is that she is a shallow, rather silly woman. Hector, it seems, is right about her, but so is Troilus since their defence of Helen has created their 'fame in time to come' without which the play could not have been written. Yet there is a further complication since, in his rejection of popular myths of the Trojan War, Shakespeare implies that their heroic reputation is itself misleading. The impression he creates is that Hector was not a chivalric soldier but a man brutally butchered while defending a cause in which he had no faith. By a final irony, Troilus and his fellow warriors have won 'fame in time to come' as pitiful creatures destroyed in a war which, in their ignorance, they could scarcely have avoided, on behalf of a woman whom, in their limited and subjective visions, they fatally misjudged.

Obviously the contrasts and collisions between different conceptions of the world are as prominent a feature of *Troilus and Cressida* as they are of *Henry IV* (where Hotspur, the King and Falstaff may or may not wholly misjudge the Prince) and *Julius Caesar* (where Brutus misjudges Antony and may have misjudged Caesar). What distinguishes *Troilus and Cressida* from the earlier plays is that problems of knowledge and judgement are discussed in general, abstract terms as well as being shown in terms of the experience of the protagonists. It is this tendency of the characters to generalise from experience which makes it, as some critics have pointed out,[20] a more explicitly philosophical play than Shakespeare usually writes. In it he makes one further development in his exploration of human knowledge and judgement, showing that, as we create our own subjective world consistently with the mind that perceives it, so we form images of ourselves consistent with the impressions we receive from others. This idea is broached in *Julius Caesar* where Cassius asks Brutus whether he can see his own face, to which Brutus gives the obvious reply:

> No, Cassius; for the eye sees not itself
> But by reflection, by some other things.   (I ii 52–3)

Cassius then proceeds to create in Brutus's eyes an image of Brutus as a man of high political principle who has a public duty to engage in the conspiracy. Ulysses ruminates on this phenomenon at more length:

> A strange fellow here
> Writes me that man – how dearly ever parted,
> How much in having, or without or in –
> Cannot make boast to have that which he hath,
> Nor feels not what he owes, but by reflection;
> As when his virtues shining upon others
> Heat them, and they retort that heat again
> To the first giver.   (III iii 95–102)

In other words, a man may possess certain qualities but can be conscious of them only to the extent that they elicit responses from his fellow men. This truth is manifested, incidentally, in *King Lear* when Lear, despised and rejected by his own daughters, begins to wonder who he actually is. It also appears when the Greek leaders deliberately over-praise the boorish, thick-headed Ajax for his supposedly gentle disposition, military prowess and profound intelligence (II iii). Ajax obviously does not match up to their extravagant eulogy, but he is so taken in by it that he proceeds to conduct himself with a lofty arrogance which, he believes, befits his extraordinary talents. He has, in his own estimation, become the very embodiment of the person he saw reflected in the eyes of others, while remaining in fact, the 'blockish

Ajax' he has always been. Ulysses supplies the general comment:

> Nature, what things there are
> Most abject in regard and dear in use!
> What things again most dear in the esteem
> And poor in worth!   (iii iii 127–30)

Here again, as in Troilus's estimate of the war and of Cressida, or as in Thersites's debased caricatures of the warriors and the impressions they actually create, there is a discrepancy between the conflicting opinions formed by the characters of one another and the opinions the audience is induced to form. In the end however what the play portrays is a series of failures derived from subjective judgements. Troilus's faith in Cressida turns out to be misplaced, the Trojans fail to terminate a war in which they have lost confidence, Hector's ideal of battle as a heroic enterprise is exploded by the brutal manner of his death, Ulysses's trick to incite Achilles misfires and, as the audience knows, Troy will eventually fall in the defence of what we have seen to be a trivial cause. The failure of all these enterprises is caused by initial failures of judgement comparable in kind to the misjudgements made by Lear and Othello of themselves and others, the result of that fallibility of perception which is characteristic of fallen humanity.

From the time he wrote *Richard II* onwards, Shakespeare created widely different kinds of drama which rest on the assumption that every individual perceives his own unique world and that these conflicting perceptions may, as often as not, result in actual, physical conflict. Conflict caused in this way is narrowly avoided in *Much Ado about Nothing* when Claudio is induced to see Hero no longer as a figure in his own callow, idealised world but as an adulteress in a world of sexual infidelity conveyed to him by Don John. The idea is obviously central to *Othello* where the replacement of the Moor's vision of his wife by Iago's vision results in the death of Desdemona. It is also elaborated with great subtlety and complexity in *Antony and Cleopatra* in which the collision between Antony's and the Roman view of Cleopatra occurs in the opening lines and is sustained to the very end of the play. An early victim of these conflicting world-views is Octavia, who is first used by Octavius as an instrument in his political schemes and is then discarded by Antony as an obstacle in the realisation of his love for Cleopatra. Cleopatra's treatment of Octavia (though of course the two women never meet) shows very clearly the tendency of all the major characters to create images of one another consistent with the world as they themselves perceive it. In Cleopatra's world, with herself and Antony at its centre, there is obviously no room for a wife for Antony and his marriage constitutes a threat to Cleopatra's picture of things. Unable to eradicate Octavia, her first reaction is to knife the messenger who brings news of the marriage and thereby try to destroy the news itself. On reflection, she finds a subtler method of disposing of her: she compels the messenger to create an image of Octavia consistent with her wishes, a woman 'dull of tongue and dwarfish' who poses no threat. In the process, incidentally, the messenger himself is transformed, in her eyes, from a 'horrible villain' to a 'fellow of good judgement'.

As in *Henry IV*, the action is distributed between two actual worlds, Rome and Alexandria, which reflect the ideals of their central characters, Octavius and Cleopatra. The one is a political and military strategist, the other 'cunning past men's thought' in the arts of love. Since Antony is required by both of them, he is bound to appear a traitor to one or the other. In his attempts to be loyal to the one by marrying Octavia, and to the other by deserting her, he is thought at different times to have betrayed both. Betrayal is, however, a charge frequently brought against the characters in the plays we have been considering: Hal appears to betray Falstaff, Prince John betrays the rebels, the Percys accuse Henry IV of betraying them, Antony accuses Brutus of treachery and Cressida betrays Troilus. In the circumstances in which Antony finds himself, betrayal and consequent disaster of some kind are inevitable. Yet the conclusion of *Antony and Cleopatra*, as countless readers have felt, is not wholly tragic and this effect is brought about in a remarkable way. Having suffered a military defeat and the loss of Antony, Cleopatra is given an entire act in which she first surveys the ruins of a world where 'there is nothing left remarkable', and then imposes on the actual world of the Roman empire, where Octavius reigns supreme, an alternative vision where she and Antony hold the centre of the stage. Her desolation begins 'to make a better life', an existence exempt from time and politics in which Caesar has no part. Dressed for her new role in the garments of a queen, instead of the chains which Caesar has prepared for her, she makes an exit (or, in her mind, an entrance) into what she is convinced will be her new existence. In her own mind she has triumphed, but in Caesar's mind he is the victor. Each, on his own terms, has succeeded. Yet Cleopatra's belief may be a self-induced fantasy, her only refuge in defeat, and, conversely, the intensity of her conviction makes

Caesar's success look like a kind of failure, for he is left in what Milton was to call 'the perpetuall stumble of conjecture and disturbance in this our dark voyage'.[21]

6 | *Dilemma and Discovery*

According to the book of Genesis, the world with its living creatures and original human inhabitants first existed in the mind of God and then became his creation. Adam and Eve were created in order to serve the will of God which they performed simply by refraining from eating the fruit of the tree of knowledge. The tree was, as Milton says in the *De Doctrina Christiana*, 'a pledge, as it were, and memorial of obedience'.[1] At first Eve is content to play her role in the eternal drama designed for her by God, but she is then persuaded by Satan that she can, if she chooses, assert her own will in a drama in which the tree will have a different function. Instead of being a pledge of her obedience to God, it will, she is persuaded, become a key to knowledge, a means whereby she herself may become like God. According to the religious assumptions on which the story rests, Eve's choice is a very simple one between good (rejecting the apple and thereby doing God's will) and evil (eating the apple and asserting her own will). Adam's predicament is, however, very much more problematical. When offered the apple he may behave as a creature in the world God has created, refrain from eating it and thereby allow Eve to go alone to her death, or he may behave as the husband of Eve, whom he loves, eat the apple and share her doom with her, a problem made more difficult because he and Eve are literally one flesh. His choice is no longer one between good and evil but between a greater and a lesser evil, between his role in God's world and his role in Eve's world, for the two roles are no longer congruent. His predicament is, according to the Genesis story, the first complex moral dilemma, the origin of all such dilemmas in a creation out of harmony with the will of God.

Having, until this moment, been at one with God, Adam decides to be at one with Eve, and in separating himself from the author of his being he obviously makes a wrong decision. But to have taken the alternative course would not have been wholly right since he would have separated himself from Eve. In a fallen world even the performance of God's will may have partially evil consequences. As he eats the apple, Adam behaves, for the moment, as if he were a free agent in a world occupied exclusively by Eve and himself. The shame which the two experience as they hear God's voice in the garden, and which they reveal in their need to cover their nakedness, is a new sensation derived from their realisation that they are also creatures in God's world. 'Shame', as Sartre defines it, 'is the recognition of the fact that I am indeed that object which the Other is looking at and judging.'[2]

Choices of this problematical kind increasingly interested Shakespeare as, from the time he wrote *Richard II* onwards, he developed a deeper insight into his characters and recognised their tendency to create their own personal images of the world. The choices they have to make are, as often as not, between two conflicting and equally demanding loyalties. In returning from exile to claim his inheritance, Bolingbroke has chosen to act rightly as a private citizen but wrongly as a subject of the King; in banishing Falstaff, Prince Hal displays his responsibility as a monarch while simultaneously betraying his friend; by marrying Octavia, Mark Antony betrays the trust of Cleopatra while demonstrating his loyalty to Rome; in halting his invasion of Rome, Coriolanus fulfils the desires of his wife and mother while alienating himself from his ally, Aufidius. For characters such as these no wholly satisfactory choice of conduct is possible. It would, according to Christian beliefs, be possible only in a world united in the service of God, of the kind eagerly awaited by Milton and other millenarians of the mid-seventeenth century whose hope was in the restoration of that holy state which had been lost at the fall of Adam. In the secular societies portrayed by Shakespeare, however, men are divided not only against one another by civil war, but within themselves, and suffer what Brutus calls 'the nature of an insurrection'.

One reason why the characters in the *Henry VI* plays are relatively uninteresting is that they seldom stop to consider what their courses of action should be. They are single-minded people who undergo very few moral struggles. Traditional loyalists like the old soldier Talbot and the Protector Gloucester know that their duty is to serve the country and are prepared to do so to the death, while careerists like Suffolk and Cardinal Beaufort struggle for power without any moral scruples. When Gloucester hears that his wife has plotted with sorcerers against the King's life, he pities her but has no doubt where his duty lies:

> Sorry I am to hear what I have heard.
> Noble she is; but if she have forgot
> Honour and virtue, and convers'd with such
> As, like to pitch, defile nobility,
> I banish her my bed and company
> And give her as a prey to law and shame.
>
> (*2 Henry VI*, ii i 188–93)

He is in a potentially tragic dilemma, comparable to Adam's or Brutus's, but Shakespeare does not attempt to develop its tragic possibilities nor does he make Gloucester's feelings wholly plausible psychologically. Again, the three sons of the Duke of York have, in principle, a choice between supporting the King and supporting their rebel father, but their unhesitating instinct is to be loyal to the family. A more interesting situation occurs when, in the middle of the *Third Part*, two gamekeepers discover the deposed Henry VI in hiding and apprehend him as a traitor to the reigning monarch, Edward IV, to whom they have sworn allegiance. When challenged by Henry with the fact that they formerly swore allegiance to him, they reply that they were loyal to him only as long as he was in power, a simple, practical answer on which the King comments bitterly,

> So would you be again to Henry,
> If he were seated as King Edward is.   (*3 Henry VI*, iii i 95–6)

No doubt there were thousands of simple, practical people who, with as little anguish of conscience, changed their religion on the accession of Mary or Elizabeth. In the following century at least one handbook was published[3] to assist men of conscience when Parliament required those allegiances which had formerly been sworn to Charles I. The discussion with the gamekeepers occupies only a few lines but Shakespeare, through Henry, notices the irony of their easy shift of loyalty and at least makes us aware that politics can create moral dilemmas, even if these hard-headed rustics have no qualms about cutting their way through them.

Such ironical situations become frequent when, towards the end of the Wars of the Roses, both kings, Henry and Edward, move in and out of office, each defending his right by royal descent to the throne and each in turn wearing the crown depending on his success in the latest battle. Their subjects are compelled to swear and break their oaths of allegiance depending on who, for the moment, is the winner. The ironies implicit in these shifts of loyalty, for which speciously moral justification can usually be found, are developed most fully in the scene where King Lewis of France is invited first by Margaret to support Henry VI and then by Warwick to support Edward IV. Lewis's reaction is much like that of the gamekeepers: to place his bet on the horse most likely to win. He is asked by Margaret to send military aid to her deposed husband, and by Warwick to offer his sister as a bride to the temporarily reigning monarch, Edward. He naturally succumbs to the persuasions of Warwick, taking care to enquire of his sister whether or not she loves this prospective husband she has never met. The ironies are compounded when news arrives that Edward has already become the husband of the Lady Grey, a revelation which induces both Lewis and Warwick to change sides. Together they resolve to join Margaret in an invasion against the King who, a few moments earlier, they were about to assist. They are guided, of course, not by a sense of moral principle, but by personal outrage at what they regard as a betrayal. Warwick sums up the situation as the scene concludes:

> I came from Edward as ambassador,
> But I return his sworn and mortal foe.
> Matter of marriage was the charge he gave me,
> But dreadful war shall answer his demand.
> Had he none else to make a stale but me?
> Then none but I shall turn his jest to sorrow.
> I was the chief that rais'd him to the crown,
> And I'll be chief to bring him down again;
> Not that I pity Henry's misery,
> But seek revenge on Edward's mockery. (*3 Henry VI*, iii iii 256–65)

The choices with which Lewis and Warwick are faced are problematical, even insoluble ones: Henry has a claim on their allegiances as a deposed monarch and a persecuted man, and Edward has a claim as a *de facto* monarch with a title to support him. The morality of their decision is therefore not a matter of which choice they make but the motives for which they make it. In the event, however, both fail to choose one of the partially wrong courses of action open to them and make what is morally a wholly wrong decision, motivated by a sense of personal insult and desire for revenge. Shakespeare is undoubtedly aware of the immensely difficult moral problems that exist in an unsatisfactory and fallen world but he chooses to present them to us objectively by creating ironies at his characters' expense. He is, as it were, more conscious of the seriousness of their predicaments than he allows them to be. They are not fully developed characters capable of feeling conflicting loyalties (or conflicting roles in different worlds) but simple characters prompted by single motives, usually selfish. Potentially tragic situations of this kind recur in these early history plays (Clarence finds himself in a similar situation, first supporting, then deserting and finally rejoining his brother King Edward), but their tragic possibilities are not pursued. This is because Shakespeare does not take us deeply into the minds of his characters, but displays them as they appear only in one mind, his own. The effect is closer to satire than to tragedy.

The change to genuinely tragic situations appears in *Richard II* and coincides with Shakespeare's newly developed capacity not simply to depict sympathetically both sides of these difficult moral dilemmas but to create them as they are felt in vividly human terms by the people engaged in them. History is conveyed to us as Shakespeare believes it was experienced by Richard and Bolingbroke and by people whose lives are affected by them such as York and his son Aumerle.

The deposition of Richard II is obviously one of those morally problematical events I have been discussing, in that Richard, though entitled to rule by direct descent from William the Conqueror, exceeds the limits of his power by conniving at the murder of Woodstock and seizing Bolingbroke's rightful inheritance. He has also, it appears, lost the sympathy of his people. Bolingbroke, on the other hand, though having no title to the throne, does have some justification in claiming his inheritance and ridding the country of Richard's corrupt advisers. He also has popular support and seems likely to be a more competent ruler than his rival. It was open to Shakespeare to create a drama sympathetic to either protagonist and there were historical accounts available to him which could support whichever view he chose to take.[4] As H. A. Kelly explains, the pro-Lancastrian historians like Walsingham depicted Bolingbroke as the saviour of his country from the corrupt practices of Richard, whereas the anti-Lancastrians like Hardyng portrayed Richard as a royal martyr.[5] Holinshed, whose *Chronicles* were Shakespeare's principal source, was critical of both men, accusing Richard of submission to 'evill counsell' and of 'insolent misgovernance and youthfull outrage'.[6] Furthermore, he adds,

> -there reigned abundantlie the filthie sinne of leacherie and fornication, with abhominable adulterie, speciallie in the King, but most cheeflie in the prelacie.[7]

Bolingbroke is portrayed, no more sympathetically, as a man who 'wanted moderation and loyaltie in his doings' and was guilty of an 'ambitious crueltie, that he thought it not inough to drive King Richard to resigne his crowne and regall dignitie over unto him'.[8] The authors of *A Mirror for Magistrates* portray Richard as monstrously self-indulgent:

> I am a Kyng that ruled all by lust,
> That forced not of vertue, ryght or lawe,
> But alway put false Flatterers most in trust,
> Ensuing such as could my vices clawe:
> By faythful counsayle passing not a strawe.
> What pleasure prickt, that thought I to be just.[9]

Nevertheless Bolingbroke is not, in their eyes, an admirable figure either, but a ruthless usurper who rules without the support of his peers and has no compunctions about sending 'a traytrous knight' to murder Richard as he lies in prison. Holinshed and the authors of the *Mirror* are fairly unsympathetic to both parties. The controversy which developed following the publication of Robert Parsons's *Conference about the Next Succession to the Crowne of England* (1594) produced opponents to and defenders of the idea of deposing a reigning monarch and supporters and opponents of both Richard and Bolingbroke,[10] but they were concerned primarily with principles and not with the characters and human predicaments of the two men.

Shakespeare's portrayal differs from the rest in his ability to treat both men compassionately, to minimise their faults and to imagine their feelings as they participate in the drama. Richard's crimes and his sensuality, of which earlier historians had supplied plenty of evidence, are deliberately played down. His complicity in Woodstock's murder, which has occurred before the play begins, is left so obscure in the opening scene that we may be unaware of his guilt; his sexual indulgences, which the authors of the *Mirror* and the anonymous play *Woodstock* describe with relish, are mentioned very briefly and in unspecific terms, and, though we hear mutterings by the nobility of his mismanagement of the realm, the only crime we see him commit is the seizure of Bolingbroke's inheritance. Beside these offences we are invited to weigh the personal agonies he so eloquently expresses:

> Alack, why am I sent for to a king,
> Before I have shook off the regal thoughts
> Wherewith I reigned? I hardly yet have learn'd
> To insinuate, flatter, bow, and bend my knee.
> Give sorrow leave awhile to tutor me
> To this submission. Yet I well remember
> The favours of these men. Were they not mine?
> Did they not sometime cry 'All hail!' to me?
> So Judas did to Christ; but he, in twelve,
> Found truth in all but one; I, in twelve thousand, none.
>
> (IV i 162–71)

Shakespeare has entered imaginatively into the mind of the man as he feels the grief of betrayal; the sympathy we feel for Richard makes questions of praise or blame irrelevant.

Again, Shakespeare made no use of the plentiful historical evidence of Bolingbroke's ambition and cruelty. His wooing of popular sympathy, to which he confesses in *Henry IV Part I*, is not shown on the stage but is reported in tartly sarcastic tones by Richard and, if his intention was to seize the crown we are never allowed to know it. His statements of intention are scrupulously proper: he assures York that he has returned to England only to claim his lawful inheritance and, even when he meets the King face to face, he repeats,

> My gracious lord, I come but for mine own.   (III iii 196)

He can scarcely appear a usurper when Richard so spontaneously submits to him. In the Flint Castle scene he claims a patrimony but is offered a kingdom. Though an audience's feeling, their pity, is for Richard, their moral sympathy can go to neither character. This is not a moralistic drama on the theme of 'the corrupt monarch' or 'the penalties of usurpation' but a more genuinely tragic work in which Richard appears destined to suffer as an inevitable consequence of his and Bolingbroke's characters, and Bolingbroke both accepts authority and experiences the first responsibilities and troubles of conscience which accompany it.

The tragedy unfolds with an inevitability which allows neither protagonist to make deliberate choices. The man who sees both sides of the situation and articulates the moral dilemma is York:

> If I know how or which way to order these affairs
> Thus disorderly thrust into my hands,
> Never believe me. Both are my kinsmen.
> Th'one is my sovereign, whom both my oath
> And duty bids defend; th'other again
> Is my kinsman, whom the King hath wrong'd,
> Whom conscience and my kindred bids to right.
> Well, somewhat we must do.   (II ii 109–16)

As the well-meaning, ordinary man of conscience, York defines the division of loyalties which an audience feels intuitively. But, although an audience is allowed the enviable position of remaining 'as neuter', York realises that both action and inaction must amount to a betrayal of one man or the other.

Bolingbroke's assumption of the throne has disastrous consequences: Richard is murdered, the country is thrown into civil war and Henry himself is stricken with a guilt which never really leaves him. Yet it cannot be said that the alternative open to him would have been wholly right. To have forfeited his patrimony and left the government of the country in the hands of an incompetent, unpopular ruler would not have been desirable either. In his situation either decision would have been partially wrong. For this reason Shakespeare cannot be said to have taken sides with either man. To Irving Ribner's question, 'What is the precise political position taken by Shakespeare in the conflict between Richard II and Bolingbroke?', Peter Ure rightly replies, 'It is doubtful whether we can ask it.'[11]

Bolingbroke's assumption of power obviously has consequences for the country which he could not have foreseen, but it also has unexpected effects on himself. In his closing words at the end of *Richard II* we get the first glimpse of the sorrow and remorse he is to feel for Richard's death but this scarcely prepares us for the picture of the exhausted, care-worn man who appears at the opening of *Henry IV:*

> So shaken as we are, so wan with care,
> Find we a time for frighted peace to pant
> And breathe short-winded accents of new broils
> To be commenc'd in strands afar remote.   (i i 1–4)

In these later history plays men make choices consistently with the kind of people they are, but their choices also determine the kind of people they become. What Bolingbroke hoped to gain by taking the throne can only be imagined, but it was surely not the ceaseless anxieties, the solitude of power and the sleepless nights he finds he has chosen for himself:

> Canst thou, O partial sleep, give thy repose
> To the wet sea-boy in an hour so rude;
> And in the calmest and most stillest night,
> With all appliances and means to boot,
> Deny it to a king? Then, happy low, lie down!
> Uneasy lies the head that wears a crown.
> (*2 Henry IV*, iii i 26–31)

This is the kind of penalty exacted from him in terms of his own personality and experience for the step he took on his arrival at Ravenspurgh years earlier. Although he does not undergo the metaphysical, cosmic disenchantment of Hamlet or Macbeth, he feels a disillusioned weariness not unlike that of Shakespeare's tragic heroes at the height of their suffering.

The course of action chosen by his son also has consequences, beneficial for the country, as he foresees, but limiting to his own character, as he probably does not anticipate. The decision he has reached before the opening of *Henry IV Part I*, and which he explains in his early soliloquy (i ii 188–210), is to make his private life subservient to his public duty, to exploit his friendship with Falstaff for the sake of winning public esteem. He also sees Hotspur not simply as a rebel but as a rival whom he intends to subject to a spectacular defeat in order to enhance his own military reputation. As he explains to his father,

> Percy is but my factor, good my lord,
> To engross up glorious deeds on my behalf;
> And I will call him to so strict account
> That he shall render every glory up,

Yea, even the slightest worship of his time,
Or I will tear the reckoning from his heart.   (III ii 147–52)

In his attitude both to Falstaff and Hotspur, he displays what Bradley
called 'that readiness to use other people as a means to his own ends
which is a conspicuous feature of his father'.[12] In the event his decision
turns out to have been a profitable one: he wins a reputation for sol-
diership by killing Hotspur, and for justice by discarding Falstaff,
but in the process he subjugates his impulses so severely that he
transforms himself into an entirely public figure scarcely capable of
spontaneous feeling. His nature has become 'subdued to what it
works in, like the dyer's hand'. We can glimpse the emergence of the
new Henry at various stages during the course of the three plays.
When, in the middle of the Battle of Shrewsbury, Falstaff offers him a
bottle of sack instead of a sword, Hal reacts like an outraged school
prefect:

What, is it a time to jest and dally now?   (v iii 52)

His sentiments are right, of course, but the tone of moral rectitude
towards an old friend is embarrassing. So is his tasteless joke over the
body of the supposedly dead Falstaff:

Death hath not struck so fat a deer today,
Though many dearer, in his bloody fray.   (v iv 107–8)

This remark is generally received by audiences with the uneasy, half-
hearted laugh it deserves: the death of an acquaintance deserves more
than a cheap joke about his girth. By the middle of the *Second Part* (II
ii), Hal is so completely in charge of his feelings that he can hide his
real grief for his father's sickness in case he should be thought a hypocrite, and his unconcern for Falstaff's feelings at the public rejection is
total. In *Henry V*, similarly, he hears of his old companion Bardolph's
execution without turning a hair:

We would have all such offenders so cut off.   (III vi 101)

The principle is no doubt just, but some sign of regret, of human feeling, would have been welcome. Although several of the low-life characters of *Henry IV*, Pistol, Bardolph and the hostess, reappear in *Henry
V*, Henry is totally unaware of them; the separation is absolute and

with it has gone a spontaneity he never regains. One kind of gain seems to entail another kind of loss, as the career of Bolingbroke also shows, and no course of action appears wholly laudable. In his own eyes, Hal no doubt appears the saviour of his country, but in Falstaff's eyes he can seem no other than a traitor.

These ambiguities persist through *Henry V* and give depth and interest to what has too often been thought a simple, patriotic play. They are apparent in what is the most moving and certainly the most overtly philosophical scene, the episode in the English camp on the night before battle. The scene is brilliantly prepared for by the slow-moving, low-keyed scene in the French camp which precedes it, and by the Chorus's hushed description of the night with the whispering voices of soldiers and the distant sounds of church clocks and cocks crowing towards the dawn. An audience is made ready to witness a battle, whereupon Shakespeare directs their wrought-up attention to a debate, the moral focus of the play, as the battle is to be the focus of the action. The debate is between the view of war seen by the King and the view seen by the common soldiers on whom he depends, for Henry has to make use of men like Bates and Williams to carry out his military ambitions as he formerly made use of Hotspur and Falstaff to fulfil his political aims.

Henry begins by expressing total satisfaction and contentment in the situation in which he finds himself:

Methinks I could not die anywhere so contented as in the King's company, his cause being just and his quarrel honourable. (iv i 125–7)

Williams's dry comment, 'That's more than we know', is very pertinent in view of the moral uncertainty of the whole enterprise, and his objection is never really answered. Instead, Bates dismisses the objection as irrelevant: as a common soldier he believes he is not answerable for the justice of the war:

If his cause be wrong, our obedience to the King wipes the crime of it out of us. (iv i 130–2)

Nevertheless, as the shrewd and solemn Williams points out, the King bears an immense responsibility on his shoulders, for he has led his men into a situation where they have little time or opportunity to prepare for death,

> some swearing, some crying for a surgeon, some upon their wives
> left poor behind them, some upon the debts they owe, some upon
> their children rawly left. I am afeared there are few die well that die
> in a battle; for how can they charitably dispose of any thing when
> blood is their argument?   (IV i 134–41)

The plight of the common soldier going unprepared to his death is,
however, something with which Henry refuses to concern himself. He
requires the loyalty of his subjects but is not prepared to repay it with
a corresponding moral responsibility:

> Every subject's duty is the King's; but every subject's soul is his
> own.

Williams and Bates seem satisfied with his answer but it is doubtful
whether a reader can be so easily convinced.

Shakespeare conveys to his audience a complex interpretation of
the action of *Henry V* by allowing us to see it through the eyes of characters with widely differing points of view. To the King himself the
French expedition is a miraculous success. With apparent conviction
in the justice of his cause, he secures national unity, wins a victory
with very few losses, acquires an empire in France and hopes to ensure
future peace by a political marriage to the daughter of his enemy. To
the ordinary soldiers, however, the enterprise is much less congenial.
In the first place their leader risks the lives of his men – and actually
loses some of them – in a cause of questionable morality. Moreover he
alone leads them into a situation in which, as they point out to him,
they must face imminent death without having the opportunity to
prepare for it. It is understandable that, in Henry's mind, every soldier should be ready to meet his end. But Williams's attitude is also
understandable: 'There are few die well that die in a battle; for
how can they charitably dispose of any thing when blood is their
argument?' In deciding on invasion Henry did not make a simple
moral choice. He tried to put an end to domestic troubles by embar-
king on a foreign war, but in so doing he risked not only the lives of his
soldiers but also the salvation of their souls.

His victory at Agincourt, as he and the Chorus see it, is an unquali-
fied success brought about by the power of God working through his

men. But in the aftermath of victory, Shakespeare shifts his perspective to the French side and, in the Duke of Burgundy's pitiful account of the ravaged land and people of France, he shows the inevitable cost of success. In a fallen world, it seems, one man's triumph must necessarily be another's failure and the same event is a cause for both celebration and mourning. Then, in the epilogue, the perspective shifts yet again and we are reminded that the empire in France, an asset in the eyes of Henry, became a liability to his enfeebled son. The feelings of a perceptive reader or spectator of *Henry V* towards its hero must take all these views into account and, consequently, can be neither of simple approval nor of disapproval. We cannot fail to be impressed by his strength of purpose, his initiative, his acumen in winning general support and his efficiency in carrying out his will. On the other hand we have to recognise his moral insensitivity, his unconcern for the souls of the men he leads into battle and his inhumanity toward the French whose land and people he does not hesitate to lay waste in order to fulfil his own personal, national policy. He is not only the inspiring leader who rouses his men with appeals to their national and personal pride, he is also the man who threatens the citizens of Harfleur with rape and slaughter:

> I will not leave the half-achieved Harfleur
> Till in her ashes she lie buried.
> The gates of mercy shall be all shut up,
> And the flesh'd soldier, rough and hard of heart,
> In liberty of bloody hand shall range
> With conscience wide as hell, mowing like grass
> Your fresh fair virgins and your flow'ring infants.   (III iii 8–14)

To blame the French for this threatened massacre is the purest sophistry.* Such inhumanity is characteristic of the man who coldly dismissed Falstaff when he had served his purpose. Shakespeare's picture of Henry shows the disinterested perceptiveness of Marvell's picture of Cromwell in the 'Horatian Ode', and Henry's behaviour in France is not unlike Cromwell's in Ireland. Both politicians are

* J. H. Walter (Arden edition, 1954, Introduction, p. xxviii) defends Henry's attitude on the grounds that he 'was precisely and unswervingly following the rules of warfare as laid down by Vegetius, Aegidius Romanus and others', but this is scarcely relevant. Shakespeare makes us think of the virgins and infants of Harfleur, not of the rules of warfare. These vivid details are, incidentally, Shakespeare's; they do not appear in Holinshed.

shown as ruthlessly successful, admirably public-spirited but deficient in human sensitivity, and both stand as examples of the kind of failure public success requires in an unsatisfactory, secular world.

It is, then, idle to praise or blame Henry for the kind of choices he makes. Faced with the prospect of either continued civil disturbances or international war, neither choice could be wholly laudable. He would, however, be a more likeable man if he were less sure of his rectitude, if he openly recognised the terrible consequences of his course of action. Brutus, in the throes of a comparable dilemma, is a good deal more perceptive about the nature of his predicament. He is, on the one hand, a patriot, a man who prides himself on his Roman republican ideals:

> Set honour in one eye and death i' th' other,
> And I will look on both indifferently;
> For let the gods so speed me as I love
> The name of honour more than I fear death.
>
> (*Julius Caesar*, I ii 86–9)

Assured by Cassius that Caesar is already dangerously powerful, he again displays his political idealism:

> Brutus had rather be a villager
> Than to repute himself a son of Rome
> Under these hard conditions as this time
> Is like to lay upon us.   (I ii 172–5)

On the other hand, the man whom Brutus's ideals require him to assassinate is also a friend against whom he has no private enmity and who has given 'no personal cause to spurn at him'. Brutus finds himself in a situation comparable to Prince Hal's, compelled to choose between the claims of friendship and those of political principle, between his role as a private man and as a Roman citizen. In the one situation, Caesar is a friend, in the other he is an enemy. By allying himself with the conspiracy, Brutus betrays his friend, as Antony is careful to emphasise in his oration, but had he abstained from joining the assassins, he would have betrayed his political principles, as Cassius reminds him:

> O! you and I have heard our fathers say

> There was a Brutus once that would have brook'd
> Th' eternal devil to keep his state in Rome
> As easily as a king.   (i ii 158–61)

As the assassination draws nearer, Brutus attempts the impossible task of remaining true to both causes, hoping in some way to destroy Caesar the politician without harming Caesar the man:

> We all stand up against the spirit of Caesar,
> And in the spirit of men there is no blood.
> O that we then could come by Caesar's spirit,
> And not dismember Caesar! But, alas,
> Caesar must bleed for it! And, gentle friends,
> Let's kill him boldly, but not wrathfully;
> Let's carve him as a dish fit for the gods,
> Not hew him as a carcase fit for hounds.   (ii i 167–74)

After the assassination, he defines with great lucidity the predicament of a man forced to choose between two evils. To Caesar's friends he declares that he was a party to the murder not because he loved Caesar less than they but because he loved Rome more. He offers tears for Caesar's love but death for his ambition and is forced to weep for the deed he has himself committed. As events turn out, the murder creates at least as many problems as it solves, but that is the nature of the world of the history plays. And we cannot positively declare that to have allowed Caesar to live would have created no problems. Either choice which Brutus could have made might have seemed disastrous in retrospect and neither choice could have been free from undesirable consequences. The same can be said of Bolingbroke's assumption of power, as we have seen, and of Henry V's dedication to the political life.

The irreconcilable nature of Mark Antony's conflicting loyalties – to his position as a triumvir in the Roman world and to Cleopatra in his personal life – is so obvious that it needs little elaboration. This is the classic case of the kind of problem we have been considering. It is imperative that he should accede to Octavius's demands for support in governing the empire, and imperative in terms of his own personal fulfilment that he should not desert the only person who gives significance to his existence. As Bullough has shown,[13] the poets and historians from Virgil and Horace onwards expressed widely differing judgements of Cleopatra. Shakespeare was in a position to select evidence showing Cleopatra either as an ambitious, treacherous schemer (Dante placed her among the carnal sinners in hell), or as a uniquely attractive, delightful, tragically fated woman. His principal source, Plutarch, was apparently her most sympathetic biographer. Shakespeare succeeded in an extraordinary way in combining within her personality an immensely wide variety of human impulses. She is jealous, violent, deceitful, untrustworthy, ill-tempered, cruel, but is also tender, spontaneous, dignified, shrewd, courageous in her death, and of course, sexually irresistible. Even her least attractive qualities are accompanied with a capacity for feeling which arouses admiration:

> Other women cloy
> The appetites they feed, but she makes hungry
> Where most she satisfies; for vilest things
> Become themselves in her, that the holy priests
> Bless her when she is riggish.   (II ii 240–4)

> I saw her once
> Hop forty paces through the public street;
> And, having lost her breath, she spoke, and panted,
> That she did make defect perfection,
> And, breathless, pow'r breathe forth.   (II ii 232–6)

Our moral judgement of Cleopatra is inseparable from our aesthetic attraction towards her, with the result that even her guile and fits of rage appear as manifestations of a uniquely powerful human phenomenon. For this reason the dilemmas in which Antony finds himself are not simply insoluble in practical terms; the courses of action between which he wavers seem to belong to different philosophical categories and therefore to preclude rational consideration.

Not that Antony ever considers his choices rationally, any more than Richard and Bolingbroke do. Totally engaged in the movement of events, he allows himself to be carried in whatever direction they, or his own impulses, lead him. A clearer view of the issues is held by lesser protagonists like Enobarbus and Octavia. Deserted by a husband who has married her for reasons of political expediency, Octavia finds her very plight exploited by Octavius as a pretext for making war on Antony. She is an innocent, abused by both men, lost in the political world which has first consumed and then ignored her, bewildered in her divided sympathies:

> Ay me most wretched,
> That have my heart parted betwixt two friends,
> That does afflict each other!　(III vi 76–8)

Enobarbus's situation is even closer to Antony's. As Antony's fortunes decline and he becomes increasingly reckless, Enobarbus is not simply uncertain whether to change to the Roman side; he is torn between the demands of good sense, which indicate the wisdom of deserting a doomed leader, and irrational loyalty which places friendship higher than survival. His choice is between the rationalism associated with Octavius and the impulsiveness associated with Cleopatra and, as in Antony's case, neither choice can be satisfactory. Crudely speaking it is a choice between dishonour and death. Having chosen dishonour, Antony's gesture in sending on his treasure, however generously intended, looks like a rebuke. Like his superiors, Enobarbus finds death the only way out of his dilemma.

Although *Antony and Cleopatra* is a play of irreconcilable worlds, of opposing personalities and ways of life, its philosophical conflicts are seldom, if ever, stated explicitly in abstract terms. Although Antony is continually under the obligation to make choices, he seldom engages in soliloquies or even, like Hamlet and Macbeth, defines the nature of the alternatives open to him. His most important decision, to neglect his political obligations and stay with Cleopatra, has been made before the play opens and his later decision to desert Octavia takes place off the stage. Shakespeare to this extent presents him as he does Bolingbroke and Prince Hal, both of whom are shown embarked on courses they have already chosen. The overtly ethical meditations of Brutus, Hamlet and Macbeth show that Shakespeare was capable of writing moral debate when he chose to do so, but he generally preferred to depict moral absolutes as we experience them in real life, not as ethical abstractions but complex experiences of the kind contained in the opposing 'worlds' of the plays, the worlds of the court and the tavern, Rome and Alexandria. Choices of this kind cannot be contained in the language of philosophical abstraction nor can the 'worlds' adequately be described as metaphors for duty and friendship or power and love. Actual experience, the illusion of which Shakespeare supremely creates, seldom, if ever, presents itself as it does to, say, the characters of Corneille, those 'experts in morality' whom, according to Martin Turnell, 'we admire from a respectful distance' and who 'sometimes remind us of a prize team playing an exhibition match'.[14] Nevertheless the moral conflicts are strongly present in the history plays in terms of character, behaviour, differences of language, contrasting visual pictures presented on the stage, and are no less powerful for being shown as physical images. The insoluble dilemmas in which Shakespeare's characters find themselves are made even more acute by the totally human forms in which they present themselves: it is more painful to see the rejection of Falstaff than the rejection of Riot, more understandable for Antony to be the slave of Cleopatra than the slave of Sensuality.

The closest Shakespeare came to composing classical tragedy of the kind written by Corneille was in *Coriolanus*, the central scenes of which take the form of moral debates between the hero's obligations to his mother and to his own principles of aristocratic integrity. Quite early in the play we are shown how Coriolanus came to be an arrogant military and political idealist. His character, like that of Henry IV, has been formed by the kind of life he has chosen – or rather the life chosen for him by his commanding mother:

> When yet he was but tender-bodied and the only son of my womb;
> when youth with comeliness pluck'd all gaze his way; when, for a
> day of kings' entreaties, a mother should not sell him an hour from
> her beholding; I . . . was pleas'd to let him seek danger where he
> was like to find fame. To a cruel war I sent him, from whence he
> return'd his brows bound with oak. I tell thee, daughter, I sprang
> not more in joy at first hearing he was a man-child than now in first
> seeing he had proved himself a man.   (I iii 7–18)

The physical transformation described in the contrast between 'tender-bodied', 'the only son of my womb' and 'his brows bound with oak' strongly implies a corresponding transformation in Coriolanus's character. He, too, has become subdued to the element he works in.

So successful has been Volumnia's attempt to shape the boy Coriolanus into a high-principled military hero that he has become incapable of acting on any impulses other than those she has instilled into him. The first challenge to his nature comes when he is required to beg for support in his claim to the consulship from the populace he has been schooled to despise (II iii 46–134). He can scarcely submit to this betrayal of his integrity, and when he is required to return to the people and plead again for their 'voices', he resolutely refuses to do so:

> Let them pull all about mine ears, present me
> Death on the wheel or at wild horses' heels;
> Or pile ten hills on the Tarpeian rock,
> That the precipitation might down stretch
> Below the beam of sight; yet will I still
> Be thus to them.   (III ii 1–6)

The scene which opens with this outcry takes the form of a highly wrought, passionate debate between Coriolanus and his mother and friends, between his aristocratic principles and their pleas for political compromise, between his role in his own world of military integrity and his role as the object of their ambitions. With the successive entrances of Volumnia, Menenius and Cominius, all begging him to swallow his pride and return to the people, the scene reaches a climax in which Coriolanus first gives way to their persuasions (ll. 99–106) but, in the very process of submission, finds himself unable to carry out their will:

>   Well, I must do't.
> Away my disposition, and possess me
> Some harlot's spirit! My throat of war be turn'd,
> Which quier'd with my drum, into a pipe
> Small as an eunuch or the virgin voice
> That babies lulls asleep! The smiles of knaves
> Tent in my cheeks, and schoolboys' tears take up
> The glasses of my sight! A beggar's tongue
> Make motion through my lips, and my arm'd knees,
> Who bow'd but in my stirrup, bend like his
> That hath received an alms! I will not do't,
> Lest I surcease to honour mine own truth,
> And by my body's action teach my mind
> A most inherent baseness.   (III ii 110–23)

Coriolanus's vision of his prospective scene with the people obviously differs from Volumnia's: what to her is 'policy', to her son is whorish seductiveness, and what she sees as 'gentle words' he sees as the ingratiating pleas of a beggar. He is a man incapable of being 'false to his nature', and when, at the end of the scene, he appears to have acceded to their pleas, we know that his true character will soon assert itself.

The principles in this debate are clearly stated by the participants and it is obvious that Coriolanus suffers a prolonged moral dilemma, that he must choose between conflicting ideals. Yet, as in the case of Bolingbroke, Hal, Brutus and Antony, we must find it impossible to decide which alternative should be preferred. This is not simply because either course is equally defensible (strict adherence to principle may be desirable in some situations and reasonable compromise in others) but because the arguments on both sides are such credible expressions of the characters who voice them that we witness a conflict as much between individual people as between the ideas they hold. The triumph of Coriolanus's will must entail a defeat of Volumnia's, and vice versa, and neither the son's implacable consistency nor the mother's ambitions for him are wholly attractive. The rights and wrongs of the situation are inseparable from the people involved in it and the principles cannot therefore be weighed in isolation from the people who hold them. If, however, we consider not the principles inherent in the scene but the specific courses of action offered to Coriolanus, it is apparent that neither can be wholly right. He must either win the consulship at the cost of his integrity or cling to his ideals and lose the consulship. The dilemma is resolved, if only temporarily, by his departure from Rome which, significantly, the Tribunes see as their banishment of him, but Coriolanus sees as his banishment of them:

> Despising
> For you the city, thus I turn my back;
> There is a world elsewhere. (III iii 135–7)

The discrepancy between two conflicting views of the same situation could scarcely be more apparent.

Outrageous and unforeseen though Coriolanus's assault on Rome appears to the Tribunes, Shakespeare shows it to be entirely logical – predictable almost – in view of his situation and the kind of man he is. His alliance with Rome's greatest enemy and his invasion of his own city is no more than an extreme manifestation of his contempt for his fellow-Romans, his confidence in his own rectitude and his tendency, which we have observed in other Shakespearean political heroes, to treat other people as aids or impediments to the imposition of his own

will. It is only when some of the individuals he is intent on destroying –
Menenius, Volumnia, his wife and his son – appear to plead with him
that his singleness of purpose is shaken. Volumnia breaks his determination by first asking him to see the situation through her eyes:

> Think with thyself
> How more unfortunate than all living women
> Are we come hither; since that thy sight, which should
> Make our eyes flow with joy, hearts dance with comforts,
> Constrains them weep and shake with fear and sorrow,
> Making the mother, wife and child to see
> The son, the husband, and the father, tearing
> His country's bowels out.   (v iii 96–103)

She attempts to awaken in him a humanity he has not hitherto displayed and which consists in seeing his victims as individuals about to
be sacrificed for the furtherance of his will and not as mere objects of
his revenge (For, like many of the histories, *Coriolanus* is also a revenge
play with none of the conventional trappings normally associated
with that mode). In so doing she defines for him and the audience the
insoluble dilemma in which she and his wife find themselves, a
dilemma not dissimilar to those of York, Brutus, Antony, Octavia and
Enobarbus. It is stated with classical lucidity:

> For how can we,
> Alas, how can we for our country pray,
> Whereto we are bound, together with thy victory,
> Whereto we are bound? Alack, or we must lose
> The country, our dear nurse, or else thy person,
> Our comfort in the country.   (v iii 106–11)

The outcome of Coriolanus's campaign must necessarily be 'an evi-
dent calamity' whether he wins or loses.

Judging from Coriolanus's reaction to these arguments, he is
unmoved by them. It is only when Volumnia appeals to his deeper
motives, his desire for an honourable reputation and to live up to his
mother's expectations, that he finally gives way. In so doing, however,
he merely chooses one fatal course of action in preference to another:

> O my mother, mother! O!

You have won a happy victory to Rome;
But for your son – believe it, O, believe it! –
Most dangerously you have with him prevail'd,
If not most mortal to him.   (v iii 185–9)

It is even more apparent in this than in the previous history plays that
the dilemmas in which the hero is placed are genuinely tragic in that,
granted his ingrained personality (which is not of his own making),
they are inevitable, they cannot be evaded, and all the available
choices must have disastrous consequences. With an irony typical of
these plays, Volumnia's ambitions for her son have the opposite result
from that she intended: in attempting to mould him into a self-
sufficient hero she has made him the agent of his own destruction.

In concentrating on these complex moral problems and moments of
choice, I may have created the false impression that, for Shakespeare,
there are no moral absolutes, that good and evil are merely relative
and depend on a character's point of view. It is obvious, however, that
Richard III is absolutely evil and that Henry VI is morally blameless,
though our reactions even to these relatively simple characters are
complicated: Richard has more zest for action than anyone else in the
play and his opponents – Margaret in particular – are almost as guilty
as he is; Henry's innocence seems inseparable from his political inef-
fectiveness and his rival, York, has much more initiative and vitality.
In creating these characters Shakespeare did not abandon his moral
judgements but, on the contrary, showed a capacity for very fine
moral discriminations. In the later histories, he guides us even more
carefully through the moral dilemmas his characters experience.
Coriolanus and Volumnia articulate very precisely the implications of
the choices they have to make, but their complex problems are similar
to those facing many of the historical characters. Bolingbroke makes a
choice perhaps without knowing it, and we see him suffering the
consequences at length; on his first appearance Hal tells us which
course of action he has chosen and we then observe the inevitable nar-
rowing of his personality; Brutus's decision requires him to murder a
friend and the appearance of Caesar's ghost suggests that Brutus's
death is a direct consequence of his guilt; Antony's impulsive deser-
tion of Octavia contributes to his own defeat and the death of himself
and Cleopatra. The tragic ironies occur so often that they appear
characteristically Shakespearean. These characters are so fully and
sympathetically created and their situations are portrayed with such

fine moral complexity that a spectator can neither praise nor blame them. He can, however, pity them in their hopeless attempts to take right actions in a world where no action can be wholly right.

7 | *The Lost Garden*

Since before literature existed, men have expressed their sense of the imperfection of the world by creating, in their imaginations, ideal worlds whose inhabitants are free from the burden of old age, the harshness of the seasons and the need to struggle for survival against nature and their fellow-men. The best known of these worlds is, of course, the Garden of Eden, the account of which conveys the belief that man was created for an existence other than the one in which he actually finds himself, that he is now a stranger in an alien land, struggling for existence in hostile surroundings, destined for death and compelled laboriously to produce those necessities of life which the earth once freely gave to him. The Christian belief in the New Jerusalem, on the other hand, expresses the conviction that man's present exile is only temporary: through faith and the grace of God he will be brought back by Christ, the second Adam, into a heavenly paradise corresponding to the earthly paradise once forfeited by the first Adam. The Christian myth of 'the eternal return' is, however, only one version of a belief which appears continually in many different literatures and religions.

In fact, the myths of many peoples allude to a very distant epoch when men knew neither death nor toil nor suffering and had a bountiful supply of food merely for the taking. *In illo tempore*, the gods descended to earth and mingled with men; for their part, men could easily mount to heaven. As a result of a ritual fault, communications between heaven and earth were interrupted and the gods withdrew to the highest heavens. Since then, men must work for their food and are no longer immortal.[1]

The Sumerian *Epic of Gilgamesh* refers to an ideal land on the other side of the world,[2] the Greeks believed in the Elysian Fields, a place free from rain and snow, where the dead enjoy eternal ease, and the Greek and Roman poets Hesiod and Ovid wrote of a Golden Age at the very beginning of human history when there was neither toil nor pain, the land was spontaneously fertile, and justice reigned without the need for laws.[3] Paradise, Elysium, the Golden Age and the Isles of the Blest are always to be found in a time or place other than the present. As one of Shakespeare's historical character remarks.

> Past and to come seems best; things present, worst.
>
> (*2 Henry IV*, I iii 108)

The Garden of Eden was lost in the remote past, the New Jerusalem may be reached in the future, the Fortunate Isles exist but in a part of the world as yet unexplored by man. They can be entered only at another time than this or in another place. A kind of paradise is accessible to us now only, as some people have believed, by a withdrawal from the world either into an inner tranquillity of mind of the kind cultivated by the stoics or by a loss of the self in the being of God of the kind described at the end of Dante's *Paradiso* and in Eliot's *Four Quartets*. Such a withdrawal, however, is not possible for the characters of Shakespeare's history plays who are compelled, often reluctantly, to apply their minds to the pressing problems of the moment.

A new impetus was given to the belief in an earthly paradise by the discoveries of new lands by the navigators of the Renaissance and the accounts with which they returned of happy communities as yet uncorrupted by civilisation. Columbus and the voyagers who followed his course westwards, observing the fertility of the American continents, the naked innocence of the inhabitants and their communal ownership of property, interpreted these signs as evidence that they had stumbled upon a Golden Age like the one about which they had read in Ovid's *Metamorphoses*.[4] The chronicler of these earliest voyages, Peter Martyr, writes that the natives of Hispaniola 'lyve without any certayne dwelling places, and without tyllage or culturyng of the grounde, as wee reade of them whiche in olde tyme lyved in the golden age'.[5] Two British explorers, Philip Amadas and Arthur Barlow, returned from what is now North Carolina with enthusiastic accounts of the idyllic life of the inhabitants:

We were entertained with all love and kindness and with as much

bounty after their manner as they could possibly devise. We found
the people most gentle, loving, and faithful, void of all guile and
treason and such as lived after the manner of the Golden Age. The
earth bringeth forth all things in abundance as in the first creation
without toil or labour.[6]

It was on reports of this kind that the most influential discussion of the
primitive life was based, the essay 'Of the Caniballes', by Montaigne,
a member of whose own household had spent ten or twelve years in
Brazil. The way of life of the natives of South America seemed to Montaigne to 'exceed all the pictures wherewith licentious Poesie hath
proudly imbellished the golden age':

> It is a nation . . . that hath no kinde of traffike, no knowledge of Let-
> ters, no intelligence of numbers, no name of magistrate, nor of poli-
> ticke superioritie; no use of service, of riches or of povertie; no
> contracts, no successions, no partitions, no occupation but idle; no
> respect of kindred, but common, no apparell but naturall, no man-
> uring of lands, no use of wine, corne or mettle. The very words that
> import lying, falshood, treason, dissimulations, covetousnes, envie,
> detraction, and pardon, were never heard of amongst them.[7]

The play of Shakespeare which was inspired by such reports is, of
course, *The Tempest*, which is also his most politically theoretical play,
a presentation in the form of a fictional drama of the essential nature
of government and the problems to which it gives rise. Prospero's
island is what the sociologists call a 'model' of human society. Its cast
of characters allows Shakespeare to portray in microcosm nearly all
the basic, fundamental social relationships: those of a ruler to his territory, a governor to his subjects, a father to his child, masters to servants, male to female and the rational to the irrational within the
human microcosm itself. Prospero's attempts to control his subjects,
both those native to the island and the arrivals from Milan, are a sym-
bolic representation of the kind of specific problems faced by the
rulers and statesmen of Shakespeare's history plays. Like them he is
subjected to fortune and to time, like them he is both a usurper
(of Caliban's kingdom) and the victim of usurpation (by Antonio); he
struggles to put down the mutinies first of Antonio then of Caliban
and his disorderly companions, and in spite of his extraordinary,
supernatural powers he cannot exact the voluntary submission of all

his subjects: Antonio, his treacherous and usurping brother, makes no response to his offer of forgiveness. Prospero's laborious struggle to restore the political *status quo* is only a partial success and the enigmatic silence of Antonio seems to remove any certainty that rebellion will not again break out, under either Antonio's leadership or that of some other envious, ambitious specimen of fallen humanity with which the play abounds. *The Tempest* is also like the history plays in its opening and conclusion: during its course Prospero attempts to solve problems which originated 'in the dark backward and abysm of time' and at its conclusion Ferdinand, a mythological Richmond or Malcolm, steps forward with Miranda to take on the task of government; the two sail off towards a new beginning as the play ends and Prospero prepares himself for death.

In *The Tempest* Shakespeare brought together and worked on the different kinds of literature mentioned earlier in this chapter, including parts of Ovid's *Metamorphoses*, the reports of discoveries made by renaissance voyagers, and Montaigne's meditations on 'the caniballes'. This last essay, as is well known, is the source of Gonzalo's speech on his arrival on the island, in which, having first remarked on the extraordinary fruitfulness of the soil, he describes how, ideally, he would govern it:

> Had I plantation of this isle, my lord . . .
> . . .
> I'th' commonwealth I would by contraries
> Execute all things; for no kind of traffic
> Would I admit; no name of magistrate;
> Letters should not be known; riches, poverty,
> And use of service, none; contract, succession,
> Bourn, bound of land, tilth, vineyard, none;
> No use of metal, corn, or wine or oil;
> No occupation; all men idle, all;
> And women too, but innocent and pure:
> No sovereignty . . .
> . . .
> All things in common nature should produce
> Without sweat or endeavour. Treason, felony,
> Sword, pike, knife, gun, or need of any engine
> Would I not have; but nature should bring forth
> Of its own kind, all foison, all abundance,

To feed my innocent people,
. . .
I would with such perfection govern, sir,
T'excel the golden age.   (II i 137, 141–50, 153–8, 161–2)

In this early speech, Gonzalo establishes himself as one of the most sympathetic characters in *The Tempest* and one of the most naïve, a quality which he shares with both Miranda and Caliban, though unlike them he has preserved his idealism in spite of his experience of the corrupt ways of civilised society. In the context of the whole play, his vision of Utopia is an account not of what society could be but of what we dream it should be, an ideal state unattainable by fallen humanity. The impossibility of his dream is apparent even as he describes it, for his speech is constantly interrupted by the cynical, contemptuous words of Antonio and Sebastian, the two corrupt sophisticates in whom his vision stirs no sympathy. His speech is not simply an adaptation of Montaigne's essay but, through the ironies derived from its context, an answer, an objection, to the essay. Montaigne compared the life of the primitive South American with that of the civilised European and doubted whether civilisation was desirable, but Shakespeare shows why the Golden Age is no longer a possibility. Life on Prospero's island is far removed from the ideal described by Ovid and reported by the Elizabethan voyagers. The inhabitants do not live 'without sweat or endeavour' but require the slave labour of Caliban to support them; far from lacking 'sovereignty' the island is governed by a usurper who has reduced Caliban to servitude in his own land, and even Gonzalo visualises himself as king of it;[8] 'use of service' can hardly be avoided when the appetite for power is so prevalent – in Prospero, Antonio, Sebastian and the drunken servants. The contrast between Gonzalo's dream and the rest of the play is not one between an innocent primitivism and a corrupt civilisation, but between a vision of prelapsarian happiness and the imperfect postlapsarian reality.

At the heart of Shakespeare's conception of politics lies the paradox that a rule of law is necessary to protect men against their own inherent savagery, yet few men are willing to be governed, and government itself may destroy the unique individuality of a Caliban (or a Hotspur or a Falstaff) which is the very quality which gives society its richness and vitality. Nearly all the characters are eager for power or unwilling to be ruled, including the faithful Ariel who longs, like Cali-

ban, for freedom. The comic servants make use of Caliban as Antonio
has abused Prospero, and Prospero manipulates everyone else as
'objects' in the furtherance of his own wishes. Even Ferdinand, that
exemplary son-in-law, apparently cheats his newly married wife at
chess, a game which is an apt symbol of the struggle for power and the
conflict of viewpoints which had interested Shakespeare ever since he
wrote *Richard II*:

> MIRANDA   Sweet lord, you play me false –
> FERDINAND   No, my dearest love,
>   I would not for the world.
> MIRANDA   Yes, for a score of kingdoms you should wrangle,
>   And I would call it fair play.   (v i 172–5)

This little fragment of dialogue suggests that Miranda's innocent
trust has already been lost and replaced by the capacity for forgiveness necessary in an imperfect world. It is the ability to forgive which
Prospero finds hard to acquire. He is frequently on the verge of
unleashing his fury against Antonio, Caliban and even the innocuous
Ferdinand. In order to carry out his plans he has to control not only
the rebels but the rebellious impulses within himself and the signs of
inner struggle are obvious as he makes the final effort to pardon his
treacherous brother:

> For you, most wicked sir, whom to call brother
> Would even infect my mouth, I do forgive
> Thy rankest fault – all of them; and require
> My dukedom of thee, which perforce I know
> Thou must restore.   (v i 130—4)

The effortlessly happy existence imagined by Gonzalo would be possible only if the consequences of the Fall could be annulled. In its context, his words call attention by contrast to the prolonged and
laborious effort which Prospero – a representative of all political
rulers – has to make in order to induce his unwilling subjects to form
some kind of stable society, however temporary. Gonzalo's dream is
an ideal by which we can measure the painful temporary, half-
successful attempts at government made by Shakespeare's historical
rulers generally.

Shakespeare depicts no unimpaired, ideal existences in his plays.
Gonzalo's Golden Age, the idyllic life of the shepherd dreamed of by

Henry VI, the life beyond death to which Cleopatra imagines she will be translated, the childhood innocence longingly recollected by Polyxenes, all exist in the imaginations of the characters. The closest approximations to them can be found in the comedies, but even their so-called 'green worlds' are imperfect. The 'shadowy desert, unfrequented woods' to which Valentine escapes in *The Two Gentlemen of Verona* (v iv 2) are actually inhabited by criminal outlaws and become the setting for attempted rape. The Forest of Arden is not a place where the exiles 'fleet the time carelessly as they did in the golden world' (*As You Like It*, I i 108); this misleading remark is made by Charles the wrestler, a city man. The banished Duke and his followers actually suffer what he calls 'the penalty of Adam', 'the seasons' difference', and our first sight of the exiled court is a group of hunters singing in defiance of 'winter and rough weather'. Like the banished Duke, the exiled Belarius is glad to be away from the corruption of court life, but his mountain refuge in Wales is no earthly paradise. He and the two princes also feel 'the penalty of Adam', the rain and wind of 'dark December' as they pass the 'freezing hours' inside their 'pinching cave' (*Cymbeline*, III iii 36–9). In spite of the simplicity of their life, the two royal children are not noble savages but wild, like animals, as they themselves admit:

> We are beastly: subtle as the fox for prey,
> Like warlike as the wolf for what we eat.
> Our valour is to chase what flies; our cage
> We make a choir, as doth the prison'd bird,
> And sing our bondage freely.   (III iii 40–4)

The pastoral retreats of *As you Like It* and *Cymbeline* are 'fallen' landscapes where men must endure the extremity of the seasons, and are not given the necessities of life without effort but must hunt and kill and cultivate the soil for food That 'best garden of the world', the land of France, degenerates into wildness as soon as it is neglected:

> Her vine, the merry cheerer of the heart,
> Unpruned dies; her hedges even-pleached,
> Like prisoners wildly overgrown with hair,
> Put forth disorder'd twigs; her fallow leas
> The darnel, hemlock and rank fumitory,
> Doth root upon, while that the coulter rusts

> That should deracinate such savagery.   (*Henry V*, v ii 41–7)

The reason for the relapse of the vines and hedgerows of France into savagery is that they are, as the Duke of Burgundy says, 'defective in their natures', an imperfection deriving from the Fall.

Burgundy goes on, after his account of the degeneration of the land, to describe the savagery of the French people and their children, and the comparison between the defectiveness of nature and the corruptibility of human societies is a common one in Shakespeare, possibly because, originating in the same first disobedience, the one reminded him of the other.[9] The comparison appears in Shakespeare's earliest plays, as when Queen Margaret encourages Henry VI to rid the court of ambitious noblemen:

> Now 'tis the spring, and weeds are shallow-rooted;
> Suffer them now, and they'll o'ergrow the garden
> And choke the herbs for want of husbandry.
>
> > (*2 Henry VI*, iii i 31–3)

The fullest development of this metaphor is in the scene in *Richard II* when Shakespeare interrupts his portrayal of the rebellion of Bolingbroke with a lecture by a gardener on the arts of pruning and cultivation:

> Go, bind thou up yon dangling apricocks,
> Which, like unruly children, make their sire
> Stoop with oppression of their prodigal weight;
> Give some supportance to the bending twigs.
> Go thou, and like an executioner
> Cut off the heads of too-fast growing sprays
> That look too lofty in our commonwealth:
> All must be even in our government.
> You thus employed, I will go root away
> The noisome weeds which without profit suck
> The soil's fertility from wholesome flowers.   (iii iv 29–39)

The garden, as the second gardener points out, represents, 'as in a model', the sea-walled garden of England whose people have become

> full of weeds; her fairest flowers chok'd up,
> Her fruit trees all unprun'd, her hedges ruin'd,

through Richard's negligence. Both man and nature have to be controlled and cultivated if they are to thrive. The purpose of government (and gardening) according to Shakespeare is, like the function of education according to Milton, an attempt 'to repair the ruins of our first parents.[10]   See bib

The tendency of the landscape to become wild and disordered is not the only effect on nature of the Fall. Evil is also manifest in the natural destructiveness of tempests, gales and predatory beasts and these postlapsarian phenomena are associated by Shakespeare with the absolute, 'motiveless malignity' of some of his characters. Richard III is called a 'biting, venom-toothed dog', 'a bottled spider', a 'poisonous bunch-back'd toad', an 'elvish-marked, abortive rooting hog',[11] and there is a special appropriateness in the fact that the boar was his heraldic device. The inherent violence of the animals, the elements and man are all combined in Gratiano's account of the rooted desire for vengeance which possesses Shylock:

> You may as well go stand upon the beach
> And bid the main flood bate his usual height;
> You may as well use question with the wolf,
> Why he hath made the ewe bleat for the lamb;
> You may as well forbid the mountain pines
> To wag their high tops and to make no noise
> When they are fretten with the gusts of heaven;
> You may as well do any thing most hard
> As seek to soften that – than which what's harder? –
> His Jewish heart.   (*Merchant of Venice*, iv i 71–80)

One way in which Shakespeare is decidely not our contemporary is in his belief in the potentiality of man for absolute evil. We are inclined, nowadays, to make the romantic assumption that, brought up under the right conditions, people are naturally benevolent and that the murderer or vandal is the victim of psychiatric disturbances caused by faulty education or traumatic experiences in childhood. Shakespeare offers no such explanations for the wickedness of Iago, Goneril and Regan. Cordelia is the product of the same stock and upbringing as her monstrous sisters.

The old Persian word *pairidaeza*, from which the English word 'paradise' is derived, signified a walled garden, park or orchard and there is evidence that Shakespeare thought of such places when he created the temporary retreats from the world into which some of his characters take refuge. There is a hint of this idea, a possible recollection of the Genesis garden, in the walled orchard of Iden, almost the only contented, self-sufficient character in the three parts of *Henry VI*. Iden's name, with its resemblance to 'Eden' may have established the association in Shakespeare's mind; the wall round his garden is the dramatist's invention and is not in the chronicle source. A royal park, surrounded by a wall, is the setting for *Love's Labour's Lost*, a play for which no major source has been discovered. Within its sanctuary the four young noblemen hope to fight successfully against their own 'affections' by living as celibates and to overcome the power of 'cormorant devouring Time' by winning fame for their scholarly achievements, a reputation which will honour them 'in the disgrace of death'. The orchard in *Romeo and Juliet*, also with a wall added by Shakespeare to the description in his source,[12] is another haven from the assaults of the world, a place where the enmity of Montague and Capulet is reconciled in the love of their children, a garden of love contrasting with the obscenities shouted by the young men in the street outside.

Iden's garden, the park of Navarre and Juliet's orchard are all walled gardens and since they seem, in their different ways, to offer shelter from a violent world, they may have been created by Shakespeare with half-conscious recollections of the original earthly paradise, or those allegorical gardens of delight which are a prominent feature of renaissance epics such as the *Orlando Furioso* and *The Faerie Queene*.[13] These havens, however, are either temporary or imperfect and offer no lasting security. Iden's retreat is invaded by the rebel Jack Cade, and the secluded academy of Navarre is undermined from both inside and out, for the Princess of France arrives on a political mission, the young men find themselves unable to restrain their natural affections and the little community is invaded by a messenger of death. The world which the young nobleman enter at the end of the play is quite unlike the carefree, gentle society of the King's park; it is a place inhabited by the dying, the 'speechless sick' and 'groaning wretches', where roads are foul and the wind blows and the sound of the cuckoo signifies adultery. The young men go out, like Adam and Eve through the gate of Eden, into a world of suffering. Nor is the orchard of the Capulets a refuge from family strife. In entering it Romeo risks his life, as Juliet warns him:

> The orchard walls are high and hard to climb;
> And the place death, considering who thou art,
> If any of my kinsmen find thee here.   (ii ii 63–5)

Like Prospero's island, these apparently peaceful enclaves have only the semblance of security: the ideal garden no longer exists.

Some of Shakespeare's historical characters, overwhelmed by present crises, look back with regret on an ideal period in the past, on what seems to them to be a vanished golden age. The first scene of *Henry VI Part I* opens with an immediate expression of loss and despair on the death of Henry V:

> Virtue he had, deserving to command;
> His brandish'd sword did blind men with his beams;
> His arms spread wider than a dragon's wings;
> His sparkling eyes, replete with wrathful fire,
> More dazzled and drove back his enemies
> Than mid-day sun fierce bent against their faces . . .
> Henry is dead and never shall revive.   (*1 Henry VI*, i i 9–18)

Very few of the history plays are without reminiscences of this kind in which present disaster is made more intolerable by the recollection of past success. Henry V's triumphant reign is again sorrowfully invoked in *Henry VI Part II* when the King makes his disastrous marriage to Margaret; there are recollections of the great Richard the Lionheart in *King John*; Hotspur, comparing Henry IV with his predecessor, feels ashamed at having helped to destroy 'Richard, that sweet, lovely rose' in order to plant 'this canker Bolingbroke'. The sense of a lost paradise and of a country falling into ruin after an ideal past is conveyed most powerfully in *Richard II*. As Tillyard noticed, Shakespeare seems to have attached a special significance to the final stages of the reign of Richard, the last king to rule by hereditary right from William the Conqueror. By various dramatic means he conveys the impression that the end of his reign is the end of an era; 'the world of medieval refinement is . . . threatened and in the end superseded by the more familiar world of the present'.[14] This effect is brought about partly by the difference between the two Kings: Richard conveys to us some of the luminousness with which he invests himself, and the restrained, unimaginative Bolingbroke is unremarkable by comparison. The play is also distinguished by its frequent, elaborate ceremonies (as Tillyard also pointed out), the manifestation of tradition and social stability; but all the ceremonies collapse before they are completed, like the banquet in *Macbeth*. The prolonged, chivalric challenges in the opening scene lead nowhere, neither to an encounter nor to a reconciliation but to a postponement, and after more elaborate, ritualistic preliminaries, the tournament at Coventry is interrupted at the moment the combatants are about to charge. Gaunt delivers a moving deathbed speech but is interrupted and carried offstage to complete his death, leaving us to hear Richard's unfeeling comments on him. The ceremony of abdication, carefully prepared by Bolingbroke, collapses when the principal actor refuses to play his part. These rituals all disintegrate because the chief participant, Richard, is either unwilling or unable to fulfil his role in them; the characteristic dramatic effect of the play is thus one of anti-climax, a dramatic image which contributes to the impression of a country collapsing in ruins. This impression is strengthened because we are also told that we are witnessing the end of a generation, that of the seven sons of Edward III, most of whom are dead before the play opens and the remainder dying:

> Edward's seven sons, whereof thyself art one,
> Were as seven vials of his sacred blood,
> Or seven fair branches springing from one root.
> Some of those seven are dried by nature's course,
> Some of those branches by the Destinies cut;
> But Thomas, my dear lord, my life, my Gloucester,
> One vial full of Edward's sacred blood,
> One flourishing branch of his most royal root,
> Is crack'd, and all the precious liquor spilt;
> Is hack'd down, and his summer leaves all faded,
> By envy's hand, and murder's bloody axe.   (ɪ ii 11–21)

The autumnal metaphor of the faded leaves is typical of *Richard II;* on the King's return from Ireland, a Welshman reports that the bay trees in his country have all withered. On delivering the lament for her dead husband, the Duchess of Gloucester retires to her 'empty lodgings and unfurnished walls, Unpeopled offices, untrodden stones', once, presumably, a place of busy life, to die.

The memory of Edward III is again recalled by York, the last survivor of his seven sons, who points to him as a model of authoritative and virtuous kingship:

In war was never lion rag'd more fierce,
In peace was never gentle lamb more mild,
Than was that young and princely gentleman.
. . .
But when he frown'd, it was against the French
And not against his friends. His noble hand
Did win what he did spend, and spent not that
Which his triumphant father's hand had won.
His hands were guilty of no kindred blood,
But bloody with the enemies of his kin.　(II i 173–5 178–83)

By the end of the play we have been made aware of a steady decline
through four generations: the shrewd, impersonal Bolingbroke has
none of Richard's magnetism; Richard appears degenerate in comparison with Edward III's sons, and beyond them there is the figure of
Edward himself, the exemplary medieval King, courteous in peace
and brave in war. It is as a patriotic military hero that Edward's
memory is invoked and it is as a fortress that England is described in
Gaunt's deathbed speech, yet another lament for the loss of an ideal.
England, as Gaunt visualises it, is a 'fortress built by Nature' against
invaders, a 'seat of Mars', a castle for which the surrounding sea
serves as a defensive moat against the assault of envious foreigners. As
Gaunt bewails the the inner corruption of his country and its King, he
thinks of England as a garden which the sea 'serves in the office of a
wall', another Eden, a 'demi-paradise' which has been ruined.
　The sense of a lost ideal is conveyed with more subtlety and power
in *Richard II* than in any other Shakespearean play, but it can also be
felt in some of the tragedies, as the critics have pointed out, and this effect provides a further link between the two genres. 'Time was' writes
Maynard Mack of *Hamlet*, 'when Denmark was a different place.'

That was before Hamlet's mother took off 'the rose From the fair
forehead of an innocent love' and set a blister there. Hamlet then
was still 'th' expectancy and rose of the fair state'; Ophelia the 'rose
of May'. For Denmark was a garden then, when his father ruled.
There had been something heroic about his father – a king who met
the threats to Denmark in open battle, fought with Norway, smote
the sledded Polacks on the ice, slew the elder Fortinbras in an hono-
rable trial of strength. There had been something godlike about his

father too: 'Hyperion's curls, the front of Jove himself, An eye like Mars . . . A station like the herald Mercury'. But, the ghost reveals, a serpent was in the garden, and 'the serpent that did sting thy father's life Now wears his crown'.[15]

Wilbur Sanders perceives a similar process of degeneration after the death of Duncan in *Macbeth*:

> Through the perspective glass of Macbeth's unavailing anguish he becomes 'the gracious Duncan', the sweet sleeper in an untroubled grave. There is no need for a putative super-nature infusing Duncan's human nature . . . to account for the haunting compulsion of the image: it is haunting because it is lost . . . This replacement of Duncan in the political order by a man of much smaller stature contributes to an overall sense of shrinkage and diminution which hangs over the concluding movement of the action . . . Duncan is the lost possibility, Malcolm the diminished necessity.[16]

The impression of a corrupt or prosaic present after a heroic and inspiring past is conveyed so frequently by Shakespeare that it assumes the features of a recurring myth of which the plays recount different versions: Cassius laments to Brutus that Rome has 'lost the breed of noble bloods' (*Julius Caesar*, I ii 151) and, towards the end of the play, Brutus complains that the idealism which inspired the conspiracy has evaporated (IV iii 18–26); on the death of Hamlet the election lights on Fortinbras, a competent but inferior successor to the throne of Denmark; on the death of Cleopatra even Octavius, another efficient administrator, realises that there has passed away a glory from the earth:

> She shall be buried by her Antony;
> No grave upon the earth shall clip in it
> A pair so famous.   (v ii 355–7)

Shakespeare's repeated portrayal of a natural and social decline resembles the ancient belief, quite prevalent at the time he was writing, that the world had been undergoing a steady process of decay from the time of the fall of man, and that its final, feeble extinction was imminent.[17] The best known expression of this belief is in the first of Donne's *Anniversaries*, but it was held by some English divines such as Francis Trigge, the Elizabethan preacher, who conveyed it to his listeners in vividly specific terms:

> The generation of man which now remaineth upon the face of the earth, is neither so big in stature, nor so strong in body nor of so many years in their lives, as were the generations before. The bones which we finde in graves digged up, which were buried next before our memories, testify the same: our skulls are but shells in comparison of them, our bones are the straws, or little sticks to theirs. And the same strength of procreation, which God gave to *Adam* in the beginning, is now waxen weake and almost extinguished, like engendering his like, as the Philosophers do say. What speake I of the decay of man? our meadowes, our lands, and our pastures testifie the same: so that every one may plainly see that the old age of the earth is nowe, and that her force faileth her, and that by and by she shall fall and faide away her selfe.[18]

The expression of such melancholy convictions may have had an influence on the Shakespeare of the tragedies and histories. More probably, however, he was portraying the natural human inclination, prevalent at all times as the myths of the Golden Age testify, to express a dissatisfaction with life itself by imagining a perfect existence supposedly lost, but which never, in fact, has been: the saintly Duncan is largely the creation of Macbeth's imagination, as the Herculean Antony may be Cleopatra's:

> CLEOPATRA   Think you there was or might be such a man
>   As this I dreamt of?
> DOLABELLA   Gentle madam, no.   (v ii 93–4)

Unlike the authors of the miracle plays, Shakespeare did not portray the exclusion of Adam and Eve from the garden on the stage, though he made plenty of references to it in the form of metaphors. The world he created both social and natural, was already a fallen world and, as the preceding chapters have shown, his characters experience, in acutely personal terms, the consequences of living in it. The dramatic images of plays as different as *Henry VI*, *Love's Labour's Lost* and *The Tempest*, however, often resemble the myth of the Fall with their evocations of the unattainable golden age, the walled garden and the ideal past. These images, whether verbal, as in

Gonzalo's description of his commonwealth, or visual, as in the scene of Juliet's orchard, whether occupying a single scene like the one in Iden's garden, or an entire play, as in *Richard II*, reinforce the impression created by the action of the plays that our world has become corrupt and that our achievements no longer fulfil our desires.

Another way of expressing the sense of the imperfection of life and to make it more tolerable is to imagine and look forward to a New Jerusalem of the future, a 'Golden Age Restored' when all wrongs will be righted. This belief, as Mircea Eliade points out, is as ancient and universal as the idea of the lost Eden: 'We find it in Homer, in Hesiod, in the Old Testament, in China and elsewhere.'[19] Visions of this kind also appear in the history plays, though less frequently than the image of the lost ideal. As Shakespeare's first history play opens with a lament for the dead Henry V, so his last history play (if he was, in fact, the author) closes with the prophecy of a future golden age under the rule of the newly-born Elizabeth.[20] Cranmer's prediction is full of biblical allusions, particularly to what R.A. Foakes calls 'the vision of a golden age that recurs throughout the Old Testament'.[21]

> Truth shall nurse her,
> Holy and heavenly thoughts still counsel her;
> She shall be lov'd and fear'd. Her own shall bless her:
> Her foes shake like a field of beaten corn,
> And hang their heads with sorrow. Good grows with her;
> In her days every man shall eat in safety
> Under his own vine what he plants, and sing
> The merry songs of peace to all his neighbours.
>
> (*Henry VIII*, v v 28–35)

In this speech Shakespeare manages to depict the perennial human need to imagine the ideal kingdom combined with the contemporary cult of the monarch (for Cranmer's eulogy includes James as well as Elizabeth).

There is one ruler, however, in whose person the chivalric virtues of courage and justice seem to have been revived and whose reign was so successful that, on his death, he acquired the status of an exemplary king. The chroniclers were unanimous in regarding Henry V as a saintly man and a heroic leader and this is the opinion of several of the characters in Shakespeare's play, including Fluellen, the Chorus and the Archbishop of Canterbury. Indeed the Archbishop specifically describes Hal's reformation on the death of his father in terms of a reversal of the fall of man:

> Yea, at that very moment,
> Consideration like an angel came
> And whipp'd th' offending Adam out of him,
> Leaving his body as a paradise
> T'envelop and contain celestial spirits.   (*Henry V*, 1 i 27–31)

Unless Shakespeare assumes we have no knowledge of the two earlier plays, however, or expects us to forget all about them, he must want us to realise that the Archbishop is deceived. Hal's reformation did not occur at the instant of his father's death; indeed Hal can not be said to have reformed at all, having been guilty of no serious misdemeanours. The Archbishop is apparently taken in by Hal's deliberate cultivation of a profligate appearance and Shakespeare is creating an irony at his expense. But the play is full of ironies, most of which challenge the legend, well-established at the time the play was written, of Henry the 'mirror of all Christian kings'. For example, after the Chorus has assured us at the beginning of the second act, that 'honour's thought Reigns solely in the heart of every man', Shakespeare deliberately introduces Nym, Bardolph and Pistol, three members of Henry's army whose thoughts are not honourable: the first admits to being a coward, and the last announces his intention to be a war profiteer. The ironies with which Shakespeare surrounded Henry's claims to be an agent of God's will have already been discussed in an earlier chapter. (See page 58 above.)

The fact is that Henry is no more an immaculate ruler than is Prospero, and his army no more perfect than Prospero's subjects. It includes cowards and rogues like Nym and Pistol as well as loyal, dedicated soldiers like Fluellen: 'no king, be his cause never so spotless . . . can try it out with unspotted soldiers'. The hungry, war-worn troops, exhausted from the encounter at Harfleur, are the best that can be mustered under the circumstances for the battle at Agincourt. Moreover, Henry's claim to rule England, and hence his claim to France, is, like his army, flawed, as he himself admits (not, of course, on his public appearances but at the only moment in the play where he is alone). The predominant feeling he expresses in his soliloquy on the night before battle is one of guilt. Knowing that his right to rule England and France is very doubtful, he pleads with God to withold, for the moment, his providential justice:

> Not today, O Lord,
> O, not today, think not upon the fault
> My father made in compassing the crown!
> I Richard's body have interred new,
> And on it have bestowed more contrite tears
> Than from it issued forced drops of blood;
> Five hundred poor I have in yearly pay
> Who twice a day their wither'd hands hold up
> Toward heaven, to pardon blood; and I have built
> Two chantries, where the sad and solemn priests
> Sing still for Richard's soul. More will I do;
> Though all that I can do is nothing worth,
> Since that my penitence comes after all,
> Imploring pardon.   (IV i 288–301)

With such a profound sense of unworthiness and with such an army, greatly outnumbered by the enemy, it is not surprising that Henry should attribute his victory to the hand of God; to the men in the retreat from Dunkirk the calm seas were thought to be miraculous. But, in the world of the history plays, no action can be wholly laudable; for one army to win, another must be defeated, and the roll-call of the French dead is shortly followed by Burgundy's poignant description of the devastation and neglect of the French land and people. Nor, as I have mentioned earlier (page 45), is the concluding peace agreement free from ironies, and the play ends with the reminders that Henry's reign was brief, that his successor allowed a further civil war to break out in England, and that he lost the empire in France which his father had struggled to acquire. Time destroyed the nearly-ideal monarch and his achievements, and Henry VI failed to fulfil his father's hopes. The life and death of Henry V, as Shakespeare interprets it, is not a tragedy but it is perceived with a characteristically tragic sense of life:

> Small time, but, in that small, most greatly lived
> This star of England. Fortune made his sword;
> By which the world's best garden he achieved,
> And of it left his son imperial lord.
> Henry the Sixth, in infant bands crown'd king

Of France and England, did this king succeed;
Whose state so many had the managing
That they lost France and made this England bleed.

(v Chorus 5–12)

'The world's best garden' is, of course, France, and the Chorus is repeating Burgundy's phrase, 'this best garden of the world'. But, if we recall the significance of the idea of the garden, the lost garden of Eden and the ruined paradise of *Richard II*, the words take on a further meaning. Henry, whatever the Archbishop may have thought, was not the New Adam nor did he recover the lost garden, but he did, for a time, achieve 'the best garden of the world' and that, under the circumstances, is the most we can expect.

Notes and References

1 HISTORY AND TRAGEDY

1. There is another possible explanation for the inclusion of *Cymbeline* among the tragedies. As the last play in the volume, it may have been added at the end simply because the copy arrived late at the printing house. See J. M. Nosworthy's Introduction to the Arden edition (1955) p. xiii.

2. Lily B. Campbell, *Shakespeare's 'Histories': Mirrors of Elizabethan Policy* (San Marino, Calif., 1958) p. 307.

3. See H. A. Kelly, *Divine Providence in the England of Shakespeare's Histories* (Cambridge, Mass., 1970).

4. Plutarch, *Lives of the Noble Grecians and Romans*, trans. Sir Thomas North; reprinted in *Tudor Translations* (London, 1895) vol. IV, p. 298.

5. See L. C. Knights, 'Shakespeare and Political Wisdom', *Sewanee Review*, LXI (1953) 43–55.

6. I am assuming that it has been finally established that Shakespeare was the sole author of *1 Henry VI* and that it was written before the other two parts. See A. S. Cairncross's Introduction to his Arden edition of the play (1962) pp. xxviii–xxxvii.

7. Aristotle, *Poetics*, ch. ix, 1451b.

8. 'Omnis comoedia de fictis est argumentis, tragœdia saepe de historia fide petitur', *Aeli Donati Quod Fertur Commentum Terenti*, ed. P. Wessner (Stuttgart, 1962) vol. I, p. 21.

9. Scaliger, *Poetice*, trans. F. M. Padelford, *Yale Studies in English*, XXVI (New Haven, 1905) 69.

10. Castelvetro, *The Poetics of Aristotle Translated and Annotated* (1571); trans. A. H. Gilbert, in *Literary Criticism: Plato to Dryden* (Detroit, 1962) p. 320. See also Trissino, *Poetica* (1563); Gilbert, p. 225.

11. The information which follows has been taken from E. K. Chambers, *William Shakespeare*, 2 vols (Oxford, 1930) vol. I, ch. ix. Lily

B. Campbell (*Shakespeare's 'Histories'*, ch. ii) discusses this same information but reaches different conclusions from my own.

12. Irving Ribner's attempts, in *The English History Play in the Age of Shakespeare* (Princeton, N.J., 1957), to trace the evolution of Shakespeare's histories out of sixteenth-century drama serve largely to emphasise Shakespeare's achievement as an innovator.

13. Peter Ure (ed.), *Richard II* (Arden edition, 1956) Introduction, p. lxiii.

14. Susanne Langer, *Feeling and Form* (London, 1953) p. 334.

15. Northrop Frye, *Anatomy of Criticism* (Princeton, N.J., 1957) p. 284.

16. See Brian Morris, 'The Tragic Structure of *Troilus and Cressida*', *Shakespeare Quarterly*, x (1959) 481–91.

17. A. P. Rossiter, *Angel With Horns*, ed. Graham Storey (London, 1961) p. 51.

18. Emrys Jones, *The Origins of Shakespeare* (Oxford, 1977) p. 119.

19. E. K. Chambers, *The Elizabethan Stage*, 4 vols (Oxford, 1923) vol. iv, p. 263; and Glynne Wickham, *Early English Stages, 1300–1600*, 2 vols (London, 1963) vol. ii, part i, pp. 75–6.

20. Sir Philip Sidney, *Defence of Poesie*, in Feuillerat (ed.), *Works*, 4 vols (Cambridge, 1923) vol. iii, p. 17.

21. Ibid., p. 18.

22. Bacon, *Advancement of Learning*, Book ii, in Spedding (ed.), *Works* (London, 1870) vol. iii, p. 343.

23. Samuel Johnson, *Preface to Shakespeare*, in *Works* (Yale edition, 1968) vol. vii, p. 66.

24. See Emrys Jones, *Scenic Form in Shakespeare* (Oxford, 1971).

2 TIME AND CHANGE

1. Sir Walter Raleigh, *History of the World*, Book i, ch. iv; in W. Oldis and T. Birch (eds) *Works*, 8 vols (Oxford, 1829), vol.2, p. 129.

2. Other ways in which Shakespeare creates this illusion are discussed by Emrys Jones in the first two chapters of *Scenic Form*.

3. The phrase is quoted by L. C. Knights as the title of a chapter in his *Some Shakespearean Themes* (London, 1959) to which I am indebted.

4. The scholars have pointed out that Shakespeare confuses Edmund Mortimer, Earl of March, the rebel, with his uncle, Sir Edmund Mortimer. This confusion does not affect my argument. See A. S. Cairncross's headnote to *1 Henry VI*, ii v (Arden edition, 1962) p. 53.

5. Geoffrey Bullough, *Narrative and Dramatic Sources of Shakespeare*, 5 vols (London, 1958–64) vol. III (1960) p. 169.

6. Northrop Frye, *Fools of Time* (Toronto, 1967) p. 15.

7. Boethius, *Consolation of Philosophy*, Book II, Prose vii; trans. Richard Green (New York, 1962) p. 38.

8. Robert Ornstein, *A Kingdom for a Stage* (Cambridge, Mass., 1972) p. 158.

9. Boethius, *Consolation*, Book III, Prose v. p. 51.

3   FORTUNE AND NATURE

1. See Willard Farnham, *The Medieval Heritage of Elizabethan Tragedy* (Oxford, 1963) pp. 104–27; H. R. Patch, *The Goddess Fortuna in Medieval Philosophy and Literature* (1927; New York, 1967) pp. 8–34.

2. See T. O. Wedel, *The Medieval Attitude Toward Astrology, Yale Studies in English,* LX (New Haven, 1920); and Don Cameron Allen, *The Star-Crossed Renaissance: The Quarrel about Astrology and its Influence in England* (London, 1941).

3. Plutarch, *The Morals*, trans. Philemon Holland (1603) p. 538; quoted in Michael Quinn, 'Providence in Shakespeare's Yorkist Plays', *Shakespeare Quarterly*, X (1959) 45.

4. Machiavelli, *The Prince*, ch. xxv; trans. N. H. Thomson (Oxford, 1924) p. 183.

5. Boccaccio, *De Casibus Virorum Illustrium* (Paris, 1520) fo. I verso; Farnham, *Medieval Heritage*, p. 85.

6. Lydgate, *Fall of Princes*, Book I, ll. 687–93; ed. Henry Bergen in EETS Extra Series no. 121 (Oxford, 1924) p. 19.

7. Milton, *Paradise Lost*, Book x, ll. 658–61.

8. A. C. Bradley, *Shakespearean Tragedy* (London, 1905) p. 273.

9. Patch, *Goddess Fortuna*, pp. 65–6.

10. For further discussion of this idea, see John Shaw, 'Fortune and Nature in *As You Like It*', *Shakespeare Quarterly*, VI (1955) 45–50.

11. *Hall's Chronicle* (London, 1809) p. 251; A. S. Cairncross (ed.), *3 Henry VI* (Arden edition, 1964) p. 150; Bullough, *Narrative and Dramatic Sources*, vol. III, p. 178.

12. Hall, op. cit., p. 145; Cairncross (ed.), *1 Henry VI* (Arden edition, 1962) pp. 142–3; Bullough, *Narrative and Dramatic Sources*, vol. III, p. 55.

13. Ribner, *English History Play*, p. 99.

14. Ornstein, *A Kingdom for a Stage*, p. 115.

15. Aristotle, *Poetics*, ch. ix, 1451b, trans. Bywater, in *Works*, 12 vols (Oxford, 1910–26) vol. xi (no pagination).
16. Samuel Johnson, *The Rambler*, no. 2, 24 March 1750; ed. Bate and Strauss, 3 vols (Yale edition, 1969) vol. i, p. 10.
17. Ornstein, *A Kingdom for a Stage*, p. 124.
18. Boethius, *Consolation*, Book i, Poem v; Green trans., p. 15.
19. Felix Raab, in *The English Face of Machiavelli* (London, 1964) pp. 52–3, explains how Machiavelli's writings were available to Englishmen. There were printed Italian editions and several English manuscript translations.
20. A. H. Gilbert, *Machiavelli's Prince and its Forerunners* (Durham, N.C., 1938).
21. Ibid., p. 206.
22. R. G. Moulton, *Shakespeare as a Dramatic Artist* (1885; Oxford, 1929) p. 110.
23. Ibid., p. 113.
24. Machiavelli, *The Prince*, ch. vii; Thomson trans., p. 52.
25. Ibid., ch. iii, p. 5.
26. Ibid., ch. xv, p. 110.

4   PRAYER, PROPHECY AND PROVIDENCE

1. Ovid, *Metamorphoses*, i 150.
2. Wilbur Sanders, *The Dramatist and the Received Idea* (Cambridge, 1968) p. 101.
3. *Hall's Chronicle*, p. 425; Bullough, *Narrative and Dramatic Sources*, vol. iii, p. 301.
4. Machiavelli, *The Prince*, ch. xix; Thomson trans., p. 133.
5. Ibid., ch. xxi, pp. 163–4.
6. *Hall's Chronicle*, p. 147.
7. Sanders, *Dramatist*, p. 280.
8. Ibid.
9. A. C. Bradley, *Shakespearean Tragedy*, pp. 340–9.
10. E. M. W. Tillyard, *Shakespeare's History Plays* (London, 1944). Ornstein (*A Kingdom for a Stage*, pp. 14–15) locates the origin of Tillyard's interpretation in C. L. Kingsford's *English Historical Literature in the Fifteenth Century* (Oxford, 1913) and in subsequent articles by scholars of the 1930s.
11. Sanders (*Dramatist*, p. 361, note 3) identifies Tillyard's views in G. I. Duthie's *Shakespeare* (London, 1951), Irving Ribner's *English History Play*, and M. M. Reese's *The Cease of Majesty* (London, 1961). To

these can be added Geoffrey Bullough's *Narrative and Dramatic Sources*, vol. III, and A. S. Cairncross's Arden editions of the three parts of *Henry VI* (1962–4). The ideas also appear in such unexpected places as L. C. Knights's *Some Shakespearean Themes*, p. 29, Northrop Frye's *Fools of Time*, p. 21, and May McKisack's *Medieval History in the Tudor Age* (Oxford, 1971) p. 110.

12. Boethius, *Consolation*, Book IV, Proses V, vi; Green trans., pp. 89, 91.

13. Tillyard, *Shakespeare's History Plays*, pp. 320–1.

14. H. A. Kelly, *Divine Providence*.

15. Ibid., p. 85.

16. Ibid., pp. 139, 159, 304–5.

17. *Hall's Chronicle*, p. 265; Cairncross (ed.), *3 Henry VI* p. 158. This crucial last sentence is omitted from the extract from the same passage in Bullough, *Narrative and Dramatic Sources*, vol. III, p. 187.

18. *Hall's Chronicle*, p. 286; Cairncross (ed.), *3 Henry VI*, pp. 166–7. This passage is also omitted from Bullough, *Narrative and Dramatic Sources*, vol. III, p. 195.

19. F. J. Levy, *Tudor Historical Thought* (San Marino, Calif., 1967) p. 176; *Hall's Chronicle*, p. 320.

20. Tillyard, *Shakespeare's History Plays*, p. 165.

21. Lily B. Campbell, *Shakespeare's 'Histories'*, p. 84.

22. Kelly, *Divine Providence*, p. 40.

23. Augustine of Hippo, *The City of God*, Book XX, ch. ii; trans. J. Healey, 2 vols (London, 1962) vol. II, p. 269.

24. R. A. Markus, *Saeculum: History and Society in the Theology of Saint Augustine* (Cambridge, 1970) p. 83.

25. Calvin, *Institutes of the Christian Religion*, I xvi 9; trans. Henry Beveridge, 2 vols (London, 1962) vol. I, p. 180.

26. Ibid., I xvii 1; Beveridge trans., p. 183.

27. William Perkins, *Works*, 3 vols (Cambridge, 1616) vol. I, p. 155.

28. Hiram Haydn, *The Counter-Renaissance* (New York, 1950) p. 464.

29. Schopenhauer, *The World as Will and Idea*, Book III, Section 51; trans. Haldane and Kemp, 3 vols (London, 1883) vol. I, pp. 326–8.

30. Ibid., *Supplements to the Third Book*, ch. xxxvii; vol. III, p. 213.

31. Ibid.

5   KNOWLEDGE AND JUDGEMENT

1. Milton, *Tetrachordon*, in *Works* (Columbia edition) vol. IV (New York, 1931) p. 92.

2. Isabel MacCaffrey, *Paradise Lost as Myth* (Cambridge, Mass., 1959) p. 34. I am indebted to this work for the examples quoted in this chapter.

3. Donne, 'Sermon Preached on Easter-Monday, 1622', in Potter and Simpson (eds), *Sermons of John Donne* (Berkeley, Calif., 1959) vol. IV, p. 128; MacCaffrey, *Paradise Lost as Myth*, p. 36.

4. For the revival of scepticism, see Hiram Haydn, *The Counter-Renaissance, passim*, and especially pp. 89–90.

5. See the article on Florio by Sidney Lee in the *Dictionary of National Biography*, vol. XIX (London, 1889) pp. 336–9; Elizabeth Robbins Hooker, 'The Relation of Shakespeare to Montaigne', *PMLA*, XVII (1902) 349.

6. Bacon, *Novum Organum*, I xlii, in *Works*, vol. IV, p. 54.

7. Mary Warnock, *Existentialist Ethics* (London, 1967) p. 24.

8. Ibid., p. 45.

9. Jean-Paul Sartre, *Being and Nothingness*, trans. Hazel E. Barnes (London, 1957) p. 222.

10. See Leonard F. Dean, 'From *Richard II* to *Henry V*: A Closer View', in Thomas P. Harrison and James H. Sledd (eds), *Studies in Honor of DeWitt T. Starnes* (Austin, Texas, 1967) pp. 37–52; reprinted in Paul M. Cubeta (ed.), *Twentieth-Century Interpretations of Richard II* (Spectrum Books, Englewood Cliffs, N.J., 1971) pp. 58–65.

11. Bacon, 'Of Truth', in *Essays or Counsels, Civil and Moral* (1597); *Works*, vol. VI, pp. 377–8.

12. Iris Murdoch, *Sartre* (Cambridge, 1953) p. 56.

13. H. A. Kelly, *Divine Providence*, p. 205.

14. Bullough, *Narrative and Dramatic Sources*, vol. IV, p. 182; and Humphreys (ed.), *1 Henry IV* (Arden edition, 1960) p. 168.

15. Ernest Schanzer, *The Problem Plays of Shakespeare* (London, 1963) p. 32.

16. Ibid., pp. 10–23.

17. This moment is well analysed in R. G. Moulton's *Shakespeare as a Dramatic Artist*, p. 198.

18. Warnock, *Existentialist Ethics*, p. 22.

19. A. P. Rossiter, *Angel with Horns*, pp. 135–6.

20. For example, S. L. Bethell, *Shakespeare and the Popular Dramatic Tradition* (London, 1944) p. 98.

21. Milton, *The Reason of Church Government*, in *Works* (Columbia edition) vol. III (New York, 1931) p. 186; and MacCaffrey, *Paradise Lost as Myth*, p. 35.

6 DILEMMA AND DISCOVERY

1. Milton, *De Doctrina Christiana*, in *Works* (Columbia edition) vol. xv (New York, 1933) p. 115.

2. Sartre, *Being and Nothingness*, p. 261.

3. Anthony Ascham, *Of the Confusions and Revolutions of Governments* (1649).

4. Lily B. Campbell, in *Shakespeare's 'Histories'*, pp. 168–212, provides a wide-ranging survey of contemporary opinions of Richard and Bolingbroke.

5. Kelly, *Divine Providence*, pp. 36; 39–40.

6. Bullough, *Narrative and Dramatic Sources*, vol. iii, p. 408.

7. Ibid., p. 409; and Peter Ure (ed.), *Richard II* (Arden edition, 1956) p. 193.

8. Ibid.

9. Lily B. Campbell (ed.), *Mirror for Magistrates* (New York, 1960) p. 113.

10. See Campbell, *Shakespeare's 'Histories'*, pp. 170–94.

11. Peter Ure (ed.), *Richard II*, Introduction, p. lxxviii; and Irving Ribner, 'The Political Problem in Shakespeare's Lancastrian Tetralogy', *Studies in Philology*, xlix (1952) 171.

12. A. C. Bradley, *Oxford Lectures on Poetry* (London, 1926) p. 257.

13. Bullough, *Narrative and Dramatic Sources*, vol. v, pp. 218–38.

14. Martin Turnell, *The Classical Moment* (London, 1947) p. 141.

7 THE LOST GARDEN

1. Mircea Eliade, *The Myth of the Eternal Return*, trans. W. R. Trask (Bollingen Series, vol. xlvi, New York, 1954) p. 91. See also A. Bartlett Giamatti, *The Earthly Paradise and the Renaissance Epic* (Princeton, N.J., 1966); and Harry Levin, *The Myth of the Golden Age in the Renaissance* (London, 1970).

2. Giamatti, *The Earthly Paradise*, p. 3.

3. Giamatti, *The Earthly Paradise*, pp. 16–30; and Levin, *Myth of the Golden Age*, pp. 13–24.

4. Ovid, *Metamorphoses*, Book i, ll. 89–112.

5. Peter Martyr, *De Novo Orbe, or the Historie of the West Indies*, trans. Richard Eden and Michael Lok (London, 1612) p. 140; and Levin, *Myth of the Golden Age*, p. 60.

6. Richard Hakluyt, *The Principal Navigations Voyages Traffiques and Discoveries of the English Nation*, 12 vols (1598–1600; Glasgow, 1903–5) vol. viii, p. 305; and Levin, *Myth of the Golden Age*, p. 66.

7. Montaigne, 'Of the Caniballes', in *Essays*, trans. John Florio, 3 vols (1603; London, 1965) vol. I, p. 220.

8. R. A. Markus points out that, according to Augustine, the institution of government was itself a consequence of the Fall: 'The origin of the servitude in which man is subjected to another in virtue of the bondage of his condition, is sin' (*Saeculum*, p. 198).

9. Shakespeare's use of images of gardening and cultivation to describe human societies is discussed by Caroline Spurgeon in *Shakespeare's Imagery and What It Tells Us* (Cambridge, 1935) pp. 217–24.

10. Milton, *Of Education*, ed. Allan Abbott, in *Works* (Columbia edition) vol. IV (1931) p. 277.

11. Spurgeon, *Shakespeare's Imagery*, p. 232.

12. See Emrys Jones, *Scenic Form*, p. 34.

13. See Giamatti, *The Earthly Paradise, passim.*

14. Tillyard, *Shakespeare's History Plays*, p. 259.

15. Maynard Mack, 'The World of Hamlet', *Yale Review*, XLI (1951–2) 517.

16. Wilbur Sanders, *Dramatist*, p. 258.

17. See D. C. Allen, 'The Degeneration of Man and Renaissance Pessimism', *Studies in Philology*, XXXV (1938) 202–27; Victor Harris, *All Coherence Gone* (Chicago, 1949); and Eliade, *Myth of the Eternal Return*, pp. 113ff.

18. *A godly and fruitful sermon preached at Grantham* (Oxford, 1594) sig. Dii verso; quoted in J. W. Blench, *Preaching in England in the Late Fifteenth and Sixteenth Centuries* (Oxford, 1964) p. 316.

19. Eliade, *Myth of the Eternal Return*, p. 129.

20. With reference to myths and religious beliefs, Eliade says (p. 128): 'Frequently, as we should expect, the paradisal period opens with the enthronement of a new sovereign.'

21. R. A. Foakes (ed.), *Henry VIII* (Arden edition, 1957) footnote to v iv 33–5, p. 175. Foakes gives the Old Testament references.

Index